Closing the Doors to Satan's Attacks:

Overcoming Fear

This book contains an Interactive Study Guide

By

Dr. Jacquelyn Hadnot

Igniting the Fire Publishing, Inc.

Kansas City, Kansas

Closing the Doors to Satan's Attacks: Overcoming Fear

Closing the Doors to Satan's Attacks: Overcoming Fear

© Copyright 2011 Dr. Jacquelyn Hadnot, Kansas City, KS 66102

All rights reserved. No part of this publication may be reproduced, stored in a retrieval system, or transmitted, in any form or by any means, electronic, mechanical, photocopying, recording, or otherwise, without the written prior permission of the author.

Unless otherwise indicated, all Scripture quotations are taken from King James Version of the Bible. Copyright © 2000 by AMG Publishers.

Scripture quotations marked AMP are taken from The Amplified Bible AMP. The Amplified Bible, Old Testament copyright © 1965, 1987 by the Zondervan Corporation. The Amplified New Testament, copyright © 1954, 1958, 1987 by the Lockman Foundation. Used by permission.

Please note that Igniting the Fire's publishing style capitalizes certain pronouns in Scripture that refer to the Father, Son, and Holy Spirit, and may differ from some Bible publishers' styles.

ISBN 0615475728

Published by Igniting the Fire, Inc.
1314 North 38th Street, Suite 102
Kansas City, KS 66102

Closing the Doors to Satan's Attacks: Overcoming Fear

Dedication

This book is dedicated to my Lord and Savior Jesus Christ. I thank you for taking the time to nurture me and guide me through the bumps and bruises we call life and closing the doors to my deadliest enemy - fear.

To my husband, Gregg, you are my best friend and the greatest support system in the world.

To the people of God who desire to close the door on their deadliest enemy - FEAR.

Let's close the doors…

Closing the Doors to Satan's Attacks: Overcoming Fear

Contents

Introduction		5
1.	Satan's Fear Tactics	9
2.	The Acts of the Sinful Nature	27
3.	Did You Know Your Were Complaining?	49
4.	I Didn't Know I Was Complaining	57
5.	Stop Praying the Problem	67
6.	Trust Got A Big Ole But!	75
7.	Recognizing the Stumbling Blocks in Your Life	91
8.	Fear: Your Worst Enemy	101
9.	Fear Not!	123
10.	Taking Back Your God Given Authority	135
11.	Is There Residue From Your Past?	145
12.	My Journey of Overcoming Fear	157
13.	Walking in Step With the Master	167
14.	Faith: The Substance of Your Life	187
15.	I'm Living the Last Chapter	211
16.	Growth Exercises	223

Scriptures for Overcoming Fear
Prayer of Salvation
About the Author
Endnotes

As a bonus this book contains an **Interactive Study Guide** at the end of each chapter

Closing the Doors to Satan's Attacks: Overcoming Fear

Introduction

The writing of this book came at a time when I was "going through." The attacks against my health started the day I completed a twenty-one day consecration. In fact, during the consecration the Lord told me I was going to go through a storm. I had no idea the storm would produce torrential rains in my life that would try and shake the very foundations of my faith. I also did not realize I was walking in fear. A new level of fear crept in slowly and without warning to hinder God's move in my life.

Every time I encounter a storm or adversity, the Lord finds a way of using it to help others. When we went through the storm in 2006, He birthed the audio teaching "In the Face of Adversity: Overcoming Life's Storms." That season moved my faith and trust in God to another level, another dimension because it was during those times when I saw God move like never before. Your faith has to grow when you see God walk on water in order to save you. Please don't misunderstand; I didn't see Him with the natural eye walking towards me. The supernatural events that occurred in my life were tantamount to walking on water. He was moving on my behalf at a time when I wanted to look down at my circumstances and not up to Him.

Here I am again putting pen to paper to share my journey of overcoming fear. This has not been an easy road for me because it means opening up places that as a human being, I would rather keep to myself. Several years ago the Lord told me that He was going to set me before the people as an example of a victorious life because the people need so see a victorious lifestyle. Recently, I revisited that statement and I must say that He is doing exactly what He promised.

The Spirit of the Lord said, "People need to see victorious living. I am going to set you before the people as an example of a victorious life."

Closing the Doors to Satan's Attacks: Overcoming Fear

Each time He allows me to go through He uses it for my good and His glory. I only write books or music when the Spirit of the Lord is upon my heart to birth out His mission. God will use whoever is willing to work for the advancement of the Kingdom of God. The Bible tells us in, Matthew 11:12: *From the days of John the Baptist until now the kingdom of heaven suffers violence, and violent men take it by force.* There will be times in your life when you will have to go through a battle, storm or spiritual tsunami in order to become the tool God uses to snatch His people out of the mouth the destroyer.

Striving for the advancement of God's Kingdom means looking at some obstacles directly in the eye and proclaiming, "I am standing on the Rock of my Salvation and I shall not be moved." One of the obstacles you will face will be fear. It is difficult to recognize the face of fear because fear is so subtle that often we don't realize we are walking in its demonic steps. If left unchecked fear can and will wreak havoc in your life. Fear, like its father Satan is no respecter of persons and it has no boundaries.

Closing the Doors to Satan's Attacks: Overcoming Fear

Fear reared its ugly head in my life through a door I left open. Because the attack was slow, methodical and subtle, I did not realize it was taking root in my life. Fear was systematically shutting down the flow of God to my destiny. I started looking at my situation and not up to God to fight the battle and bring the victory in my life.

Satan doesn't launch a full frontal attack with fear; he slowly insinuates fear into your life one drop at a time. The first drop started with a building and almost cost me Igniting the Fire Media Group's destiny.

Fear is designed to shut you down. The cost of fear is high and the end result of fear can permeate every area of your life. That is why it is imperative that we close the doors to Satan's attacks and overcome fear.

I pray that this book will enlighten you concerning the tactics of Satan, the ultimate fear monger.

Let's close the doors!

Chapter 1
Satan's Fear Tactics

As children of God, we have two choices: we can choose to walk in fear or we can choose to walk in faith. The choices appear simple, but in reality pose monumental questions to the believer. For example, how do I walk in faith? How do I know when I am walking in fear? Is my faith in God's promises sure? Is the foundation on which I am standing rooted and grounded in Christ? Am I walking in the fruits of the Spirit? The answer is found in the following verse of Psalm 139:23, *Search me, O God, and know my heart: try me, and know my thoughts.*

Daily we face situations that challenge our faith. If we leave the situations unchecked, they will wreak havoc in our lives. They will grow from minor annoyances to full-blown problems. The result, the enemy finds a crack in our foundation. Once he has discovered a crack in our foundation, he can begin a campaign against us. He is very legalistic and therefore knows his rights.

Closing the Doors to Satan's Attacks: Overcoming Fear

His legal rights say, this person has trespassed into my territory and therefore, I [Satan] have a right to send my demonic forces to attack his finances, health, marriage, children, employment, ministry, faith, etc.

Satan understands his rights and the rules of engagement. He knows that once the believer begins to walk in the demonic fruits of his spirit, he can legally launch his attack.

> *Now the works of the flesh are manifest, which are these; Adultery, fornication, uncleanness, lasciviousness, Idolatry, witchcraft, hatred, variance, emulations, wrath, strife, seditions, heresies, Envyings, murders, drunkenness, revellings* (Galatians 5:19-21).

When we allow the fruits of the enemy to operate in our lives, what are we saying to God? Are we saying that we trust the enemy more than we trust God? Are we allowing Satan the author of fear to rule our lives? Why are we

Closing the Doors to Satan's Attacks: Overcoming Fear

allowing fear, doubt or unbelief to operate? The Bible says in Second Timothy 1:7, *For God hath not given us the spirit of fear; but of power, and of love, and of a sound mind.*

Satan can smell fear, pride, envy, or un-forgiveness on a believer's heart. He can smell his fruit because he is the father of the works of the sinful nature. A father knows his child and Jesus said in John 8:44, *you belong to your father, the devil, and you want to carry out your father's desire. He was a murderer from the beginning, not holding to the truth, for there is no truth in him. When he lies, he speaks his native language, for he is a liar and the father of lies.*

When Satan smells fear in the heart of the believer, he will use fear to bring about doubt. Once doubt sets in, he can then insert negativity and when you combine: fear, doubt and negativity - the believer no longer trusts in the promises of God and his destiny is hindered.

Closing the Doors to Satan's Attacks: Overcoming Fear

When Satan smells pride in the heart of the believer, he will use pride to bring about arrogance, conceit, feelings of self-importance and finally a total dependence on SELF. One of the biggest enemies of your walk with the Lord is your **SELF-LIFE.** Your **self-life** is your will, your thoughts and your desires that differ from God's purpose for your life. God has a purpose and destiny for our lives, but He is not going to force you to walk into your destiny, He has given us free will.*[1]*

When Satan smells envy in the heart of the believer, he will use envy to bring about jealousy, covetousness, and greed. When Satan smells un-forgiveness in the heart of the believer, he will use un-forgiveness to sow seeds of discord, anger, resentment and often rebellion.

There are two doors to choose from, the door of fear or the door of faith. The door of fear can appear larger than life. While at the same time more subtle than the door of faith. The door of fear can also seem impossible to handle because we don't understand its elements. The believer

Closing the Doors to Satan's Attacks: Overcoming Fear

feels overwhelmed by the insurmountable odds standing at the door called fear.

We are faced with more months at the end of our money. In other words, we cannot pay our bills. We see the sickness in our loved ones eyes. We watch as our children spiral out of control and succumb to the pressure from peers. We cry ourselves to sleep as our marriages disintegrate. With so many overwhelming obstacles facing us, it is no wonder the door of fear appears as a giant towering over us ready to crush us at any moment.

The storms of life will come in like floods of raging waters, but the Lord makes us a promise in Isaiah 59:19: *When the enemy shall come in like a flood, the spirit of the LORD shall lift up a standard against him.*

We can see God's promise in Isaiah 59:19, so why is it that we do not stand on the promise? Why do we allow the enemy to speak to us and bring about fear and doubt? Could it be due to unbelief? Unbelief is a hindrance to

Closing the Doors to Satan's Attacks: Overcoming Fear

the power of God in your life. Not only does it stop the flow of God's power, it also stops the flow of God's blessings.

It binds the individual to a life of mediocrity. Unbelief is equal to rebellion and we cannot enter into the presence of the Lord with unbelief or rebellion on our hearts. Belief requires faith and without faith, it is impossible to please God. *And without faith it is impossible to please God, because anyone who comes to him must believe that he exists and that he rewards those who earnestly seek him* (Hebrews 11:6).[2]

When we walk in unbelief, we will suffer the pains associated with it. We will suffer fear, doubt, negativity and the like. The result, we settle for a life of mediocrity. Hebrews 3:8-19 states: *...do not harden your hearts as you did in the rebellion, during the time of testing in the desert, where your fathers tested and tried me and for forty years saw what I did. That is why I was angry with that generation, and I said, 'Their hearts are always*

Closing the Doors to Satan's Attacks: Overcoming Fear

going astray, and they have not known my ways.' So I declared on oath in my anger, 'They shall never enter my rest.'" See to it, brothers, that none of you has a sinful, unbelieving heart that turns away from the living God. But encourage one another daily, as long as it is called today, so that none of you may be hardened by sin's deceitfulness. We have come to share in Christ if we hold firmly till the end the confidence we had at first. As has just been said: "Today, if you hear his voice, do not harden your hearts as you did in the rebellion." Who were they who heard and rebelled? Were they not all those Moses led out of Egypt? And with whom was he angry for forty years? Was it not with those who sinned, whose bodies fell in the desert? And to whom did God swear that they would never enter his rest if not to those who disobeyed? So we see that they were not able to enter, because of their unbelief.

When we hear the voice of the Lord, we should act upon His directives immediately. Our hearts should be so tender towards the Lord that we move in total faith and

Closing the Doors to Satan's Attacks: Overcoming Fear

obedience to His will and plan for us. It is dangerous to become hardened by sin's deceitfulness. Therefore, we must not be as the children of Israel, having heard, rebelled. We must, as partakers of Christ hold the beginning of our confidence steadfast to the end.

Our prayer should be, *teach me Your way, O Lord, and lead me in a plain and even path because of my enemies [those who lie in wait for me].* (Psalm 27:11 AMP). Your enemy is Satan, the father of lies, fear and unbelief. The enemy lies in wait for the moment when he can kill your joy, steal your blessings, and rob you of your destiny in Christ Jesus.

While the enemy lies in wait for his prey, he sets a trap to ensnare the believer into his web of deceit, lies and manipulations. Because the believer has partaken of his fruit, Satan knows the right places to strike his prey.

This is war and it is not fought in the natural realm it is fought in the spirit realm. Ephesians 6:12 makes this clear, *for we wrestle not against flesh and blood, but against principalities, against powers, against the rulers of the darkness of this world, against spiritual wickedness in high places.*

Galatians 5:16-26 draws a clear contrast between the lifestyle of the Spirit filled believer and that of the person controlled by the sinful nature. The Apostle Paul discusses general lifestyle differences by emphasizing that the Spirit and the sinful nature are at war with each other. He also discusses a specific list of both the acts of the sinful nature and the fruit of the Spirit.

But I say, walk by the Spirit, and you will not carry out the desire of the flesh. For the flesh sets its desire against the Spirit, and the Spirit against the flesh; for these are in opposition to one another, so that you may not do the things that you please. But if you are led by the Spirit, you are not under the Law. Now the deeds of the flesh are evident, which are: immorality, impurity, sensuality, idolatry,

> *sorcery, enmities, strife, jealousy, outbursts of anger, disputes, dissensions, factions, envying, drunkenness, carousing, and things like these, of which I forewarn you, just as I have forewarned you, that those who practice such things will not inherit the kingdom of God. But the fruit of the Spirit is love, joy, peace, patience, kindness, goodness, faithfulness, gentleness, self-control; against such things there is no law. Now those who belong to Christ Jesus have crucified the flesh with its passions and desires. If we live by the Spirit, let us also walk by the Spirit. Let us not become boastful, challenging one another, envying one another* (Galatians 5:16-26).

The New Scofield Study Bible's interpretative notes give us this definition of the sinful nature of flesh:

> *Flesh is your sinful nature and in the ethical sense is the whole natural or unregenerate individual – spirit, soul, and body – as centered on self, prone to sin, and opposed to God. Romans 7:18 says of us,*

Closing the Doors to Satan's Attacks: Overcoming Fear

for I know that in me (that is, in my flesh,) dwelleth no good thing: for to will is present with me: but how to perform that which is good I find not. The regenerate individual is not controlled by the flesh (sinful nature) but the flesh (sinful nature) is still in him and he may, according to his choice, "carry out the desire of the flesh" or "walk by the Spirit." In the first case he is a "worldly" Christian, in the second, a "spiritual" Christian. Victory over the flesh will be the habitual experience of the Christian who walks in the Spirit.[3]

Look at terms that define the sinful nature. Terms such as being *"in the flesh"* or *"to be carnally minded"* are terms for the sinful (human) nature. The sinful nature remains within Christians after their conversion and is our deadliest enemy. We must die daily to the sinful human nature if we are to walk by the Spirit.

Look at Romans 8:6-8, 13 and what it has to say about our deadliest enemy:

Closing the Doors to Satan's Attacks: Overcoming Fear

For to be carnally minded is death; but to be spiritually minded is life and peace. Because the carnal mind is enmity against God: for it is not subject to the law of God, neither indeed can be. So then they that are in the flesh cannot please God (Romans 8:6-8). *For if ye live after the flesh, ye shall die: but if ye through the Spirit do mortify the deeds of the body, ye shall live* (Romans 8:13).

Also, Galatians 5:17 and 21:

For the flesh lusteth against the Spirit, and the Spirit against the flesh: and these are contrary the one to the other: so that ye cannot do the things that ye would (Galatians 5:17). *...They which do such things shall not inherit the kingdom of God* (Galatians 5:21).

When you understand how the lusts of the flesh can open doors for Satan's attacks, you can begin the journey of closing the doors to his attacks by addressing the root causes of the attack.

Closing the Doors to Satan's Attacks: Overcoming Fear

I have discovered an important fact over the years and the fact is that people cannot solve problems they do not understand. You cannot change a behavior that you do not realize is killing you, physically, spiritually, financially or emotionally. We must never assume that people, simply because they profess Christ, truly understand the depths of what is required to live a fulfilling Christian life.

A woman made a statement that I believe many of us have faced at some point in our Christian walk. She said, *"It took a long time for me to understand this Christian walk. I thought that when I was saved I could continue going to the clubs on Saturday and attend church on Sunday. The only thing that changed is what I did on Sunday morning. No one told me to change my lifestyle."*

I can relate to her statement because in the 80's when I was "saved" I didn't see anything wrong with smoking marijuana and going to church. I was a faithful tither, attended every Sunday, did not miss an evening service and drank like a sailor. *(Time to spit truth.)*

Closing the Doors to Satan's Attacks: Overcoming Fear

The revelation of God's requirements for my life had absolutely no relevance in my mind or on my heart. I gave him what I thought he wanted: a confession with my mouth, but not with my heart. I continued to walk in the fruits of Satan the deceiver. I had my own version of righteousness because I was ignorant of Satan's devices.

For not knowing about God's righteousness and seeking to establish their own, they did not subject themselves to the righteousness of God (Romans 10:3).

Let's establish a clear definition for each of the fruits of Satan's evil spirit. When you understand your enemy, you can better stand against him in times of trouble. Satan's plan is to keep you ignorant of his devices. Jesus said in Second Corinthians 2:11, *to keep Satan from getting the advantage over us; for we are not ignorant of his wiles and intentions* (AMP).

Closing the Doors to Satan's Attacks: Overcoming Fear

We are also told in First Corinthians 6:9-10: *Know ye not that the unrighteous shall not inherit the kingdom of God? Be not deceived: neither fornicators, nor idolaters, nor adulterers, nor effeminate, nor abusers of themselves with mankind, Nor thieves, nor covetous, nor drunkards, nor revilers, nor extortioners, shall inherit the kingdom of God* (KJV).

Therefore, *do not be deceived, God is not mocked; for whatever a man sows, this he will also reap.*

(Galatians 6:7)

> Close the book and seek God for the answers to the questions in the study guide section for Chapter 1.

There is no fear in love; but perfect love casteth out fear: because fear hath torment. He that feareth is not made perfect in love.
1John 4:18

Closing the Doors to Satan's Attacks: Overcoming Fear

Satan's Fear Tactics
Interactive Study Guide
Chapter 1

1. As children of God, we have two choices: we can choose to walk in fear or we can choose to:

   _____
   _____
   _____

2. Psalm 139:23:

   _____
   _____
   _____

3. What are two doors for us to choose, the door of fear or

   _____

4. When Satan smells envy in the heart of the believer, he will use envy to bring about _____, covetousness, and greed. When Satan smells

Closing the Doors to Satan's Attacks: Overcoming Fear

_____ in the heart of the believer, he will use un-forgiveness to sow seeds of discord, anger, resentment and often rebellion.

5. End the chapter in prayer before going to the exercise. Exercise: Stop reading and close the book and begin to seek the Lord for doors that you have left open for Satan's attacks. As He begins to reveal open doors to you, write down His revelation and instructions for closing the door.

_____
_____
_____
_____
_____
_____
_____
_____
_____

Chapter 2
The Acts of the Sinful Nature

> As you read chapter two pause for a moment and take a spiritual inventory. A spiritual inventory is one of the first steps to addressing areas left open for Satan's attacks.
>
> It may not be pretty and it certainly won't be comfortable - let's face it exposing sin never is, but it is real and necessary for your spiritual growth. GOT PAPER?

Look at the acts of the sinful nature aka Satan's evil fruit.

1. **Adultery** - (Greek-*porneia*) sexual activity or intercourse outside of marriage. The word pornography comes from the root porneia and thus sexual immorality comprehensively may include taking pleasure in pornographic pictures, films or writings (Exodus 20:14; Matt. 5:31-32; 19:9; 1 Corinthians 5:1).

2. **Fornication** - (Gk-*akatharsia*) sexual sins, evil deeds and vices, including thoughts and desires of the heart (Acts 15:20, 29; 21:25; Eph. 5:3; Col. 3:5).

3. **Uncleanness & lasciviousness** - (Gk-*aselgeia*) sensuality; following one's passions and desires of the heart (2 Corinthians 12:21).

4. **Idolatry** - (Gk-*eidelolatria*) Worship of spirits, persons or graven images; trust in any person, institution or thing as having equal or greater authority than God and His Word (Col. 3:5).

5. **Witchcraft** - (Gk-*pharmakeia*) sorcery, spiritism, black magic, worship of demons and use of drugs to produce "spiritual" experience (Exodus 7:11, 22; 8:18; Revelation 9:21; 18:23).

6. **Hatred** - (Gk-*echthra*) intense, hostile intentions and acts; extreme dislike.

7. **Variance** - (Gk-*eris*) quarreling, antagonism; struggle for superiority (Romans 1:29; 1 Corinthians 1:11; 3:3).

8. **Emulations** - (Gk-*zelos*) resentfulness, envy of another's success.

9. **Wrath** - (Gk-*thumos*) explosive anger that flames into violent words or deeds (Colossians 3:8).

10. **Strife** - (Gk-*eritheia*) unrighteous seeking power or position (2 Corinthians 12:20; Phil. 1:16-17).

11. **Seditions** - (Gk-dichostasia) introducing divisive teachings not supported by God's Word (Romans 16:17).

12. **Heresies** - (Gk-*hairesis*) unorthodox religious opinion: an opinion or belief that contradicts established religious teaching, especially one that is officially condemned by a religious authority.

13. **Envying** - (Gk-*phthonos*) resentful dislike of another person who has something that one desires. (Romans 13:13; 1 Corinthians 3:3)

14. **Drunkenness** - (Gk-*methe*) impairing one's mental or physical control by alcoholic drink.

15. **Revellings** - (Gk-*Komos*) excessive feasting and revelry; a party spirit involving alcohol, drugs, sex or the like.

When the Spirit of the Lord begins to reveal your sinful nature, it is vital to seek forgiveness immediately. We should respond like Job in Job 34:32: *Teach me what I do not see [in regard to how I have sinned]; if I have done iniquity, I will do it no more (AMP)?*

When the Lord begins to reveal sins that have been buried deep in the recesses of your mind, you will find that it is an ugly, foul smelling sight. Horrendous sins we committed in the eyes of Almighty God. Sins we thought

Closing the Doors to Satan's Attacks: Overcoming Fear

no one saw, but God saw and it was a stench in His nostrils.

Unfortunately, many of us never realized the sins we committed in the 70's, 80's or 90's were lying dormant just waiting for Satan to throw them in our faces. The season in which God begins to raise us to walk into our destiny and purpose is the season Satan will begin to accuse us of our past. Un-confessed sins have a way of resurrecting when you least expect it. We must ask the Lord daily to search our hearts and our thoughts to determine if He finds sin and iniquity in us. Our desire must be for the Lord to lead us on a straight path of righteousness, burning out everything along the path that is not like Him.

Recently, the Lord called me to a twenty-one day consecration. The Spirit of the Lord said, *"you are about to enter your twenty one day consecration, when you walk out you will walk out with clarity of purpose."* During the journey, the Lord spoke about many things and

Closing the Doors to Satan's Attacks: Overcoming Fear

I kept a journal of the deep treasures He shared with me. As I came to the end of my journey, He began to deal with me about the sins of my past. My past sins became compressed and compacted like vacuum-packed coffee. I went to the cupboard and took out a package of coffee. This is what the Lord showed me:

We have compacted so much into our everyday lives that we have left little room for God. Three day, seven day, fourteen day, or twenty-one day fasts that are singularly inclusive of God are nearly impossible.

We abstain from food, sex, television, etc. but for the most part, we continue the other compacted day-to-day activities. Therefore, the chance for an encounter, an intimate encounter with God becomes in reality - a stolen moment. Although we are fasting for more of God, we are in fact robbing ourselves of the most exciting chance to be with God. Daily routines are just that--daily [habits.]

Closing the Doors to Satan's Attacks: Overcoming Fear

We have been programmed by life - not by God. For the most part we have a very rigid agenda - we call **LIFE**.

1. Work
2. Children
3. Home (grass, laundry, television, telephone)
4. Church (Sunday & Wednesday)
5. Sleep 6 to 8 hours.

The Spirit of the Lord went on to say, *"There is so much that I want to give my children, but they give so little of themselves. Where is the sacrifice? When man begins to de-clutter his life, then he can make room for me. Intimacy with me is not occasional - it is a lifestyle. Man misses me due to lack of intimacy."*

[**Reflection**: The spirit of the Lord cannot speak to us about our hidden sins if we are not in a place of intimacy with Him.]

Closing the Doors to Satan's Attacks: Overcoming Fear

The Spirit of the Lord continued speaking, *"You will begin to see those that are great in the eyes of man begin to fall. Do not be surprised or amazed because I told you I was going to pull back the covers and expose the filthy and vile things they are doing in my name. The abominations will continue to grow, but they have only just begun. Man has strayed from me in his heart. There are those who have distanced themselves from me believing they are doing my work, praying with an empty heart and lying to themselves. Until the leadership is humble and broken, the people will remain indifferent to me."*

Finally, the Lord said, *"Tell my people to clean up their lives so there is room for me. The house must be clean; I will not dwell in an unclean thing."*

I pray that this powerful word from the Lord saturates your spirit and you receive His message with great clarity. It was a revelation for me - a reality check.

Closing the Doors to Satan's Attacks: Overcoming Fear

[**Reflection**: During my twenty one-day consecration, the Lord instructed me to do the following each morning. To anoint myself with oil each morning as I showered and pray Psalm 51. This was His explanation.]

"Do you know why I said bathe and anoint yourself with oil? Because I want you to begin each day, clean and purged in heart. Your cleansing is a symbol of surrender, repentance and restoration. Nevertheless, each day it begins anew. Like My mercies begin new each day - man sins daily. Man must be cleansed in the Blood daily through repentance for his sins."

The Spirit of the Lord concluded with this revelation: This is where it gets deep.

"When man fails to pray and ask for forgiveness of sins - sin like dead skin will begin to accumulate.

Closing the Doors to Satan's Attacks: Overcoming Fear

When this happens, it becomes a stench to the body, the physical body. Man must bathe daily to avoid body odor. It is the same with repentance; man must repent daily if he is to be washed in My Blood. The stench of un-repented sin hinders prayers.

> If my people, which are called by my name, shall humble themselves, and pray, and seek my face, and turn from their wicked ways; then will I hear from heaven, and will forgive their sin, and will heal their land (2 Chronicles 7:14).

As you wash daily in anointing oil you are symbolically being purged. This is a reminder to you that I require this of those that belong to me."

As I walked out my new journey of learning the keys to repentance, the Lord took me deeper into understanding the need for repentance. Rapid radical repentance is the key to killing the self-life issues of the flesh; it also goes deeper into the un-confessed sins of our past. As you

Closing the Doors to Satan's Attacks: Overcoming Fear

acknowledge your self-life issues; you are on the right road to taking a spiritual inventory of yourself. Our spiritual inventory might take us back 20 years, but I am a living witness it is worth every agonizing moment.

Unfortunately, many believers carry around baggage from the past never realizing the weight they unnecessarily drag through life. The excess baggage is harmful to every aspect of our lives. It will hinder the fullness of God working in and through us.

The Lord showed me the un-confessed sins of my past and the depths Satan was going to in order to keep me from my destiny. The enemy used my past to keep a door open to my health. He would systematically shut me down with headaches every time I began to walk into my destiny. While in the shower one morning the Lord brought to my remembrance sins committed in my youth. Initially, I didn't understand why the memories came rushing back, but the Lord in His infinite wisdom explained that He was putting me in remembrance of un-

Closing the Doors to Satan's Attacks: Overcoming Fear

confessed sins from my past that were still on the spiritual books. I needed to repent so that He could blot out my transgressions. *"I, even I, am he who blots out your transgressions, for my own sake, and remembers your sins no more. Review the past for me, let us argue the matter together; state the case for your innocence."* (Isaiah 43:25-26 AMP).

This is an example I'm sure many of us can relate. In our teenage years, we encountered people that left a lasting impression. Some of the lasting impressions were seeds of fear, anger or un-forgiveness. Unfortunately, we did not realize seeds were being planted while we were young. We went on to college, marriage, careers and families. When the time came to attend the high school reunion, thoughts reflected back to the horrible treatment by the quarterback of the football team, the girl who humiliated you in the bathroom, or the fact that you still hate your first crush for dumping you. When the thought of seeing people from your past makes you sick - check your flesh you might be holding on to un-forgiveness.

Closing the Doors to Satan's Attacks: Overcoming Fear

If this is in any way a reality check, seek the Lord for the crack in your foundation. He will reveal it to you. Your heart's cry must be a reflection of Psalm 139:

O LORD, you have searched me and you know me. You know when I sit and when I rise; you perceive my thoughts from afar. You discern my going out and my lying down; you are familiar with all my ways (Psalm 139:1-3). *Search me, O God, and know my heart; test me and now my anxious thoughts. See if there is any offensive way in me, and lead me in the way everlasting* (Psalm 139:23-24).

With each passing day, we draw closer to the Lord's return. There is a great work ahead if we are to fulfill the great commission as set forth by Jesus Christ. If we remain in an unrepentant state, Satan's doors and inroads will hinder our work for God's Kingdom. We are mandated to fulfill the great commission.

And Jesus came and spake unto them, saying, All power is given unto me in heaven and in earth. Go

Closing the Doors to Satan's Attacks: Overcoming Fear

ye therefore, and teach all nations, baptizing them in the name of the Father, and of the Son, and of the Holy Ghost: Teaching them to observe all things whatsoever I have commanded you: and, lo, I am with you always, even unto the end of the world. Amen (Matthew 28:18-20).

To go a step deeper we are also called to be restorers of the breach...

And they that shall be of thee shall build the old waste places: thou shalt raise up the foundations of many generations; and thou shalt be called, The repairer of the breach, The restorer of paths to dwell in (Isaiah 58:12).

Broken people cannot restore broken people and unfortunately, hurting people will hurt other people. God must heal us first, if we are to become effective vessels for the Master's use. Restoration will only occur when we begin to take a spiritual inventory of our lives and seek the

Closing the Doors to Satan's Attacks: Overcoming Fear

Lord for the broken, desolate or hidden places buried within us.

> Close the book and seek God for the answers to the questions in the study guide section for chapter 2

So that we may boldly say, The Lord is my helper, and I will not fear what man shall do unto me.

Heb 13:6

Chapter 2
The Acts of the Sinful Nature
Study Guide

1. What are the acts of the sinful nature?

_____
_____
_____
_____
_____
_____
_____
_____
_____
_____
_____
_____
_____
_____
_____
_____

Closing the Doors to Satan's Attacks: Overcoming Fear

Closing the Doors to Satan's Attacks: Overcoming Fear

2. When God reveals sinful acts in us we should respond like Job in Job 34:32:

Closing the Doors to Satan's Attacks: Overcoming Fear

3. What does Job 34:32 speak to your heart?

_____
_____
_____
_____
_____
_____
_____
_____
_____

4. Write out Isaiah 58:12:

_____
_____
_____
_____
_____
_____
_____
_____
_____

Closing the Doors to Satan's Attacks: Overcoming Fear

5. Ask the Lord to reveal any broken, desolate or hidden places in you. Ask Him to reveal any areas that are open doors to Satan's attacks.

Chapter 3
Did You Know Your Were Complaining?

One of the worst enemies of your prayer life is a complaining spirit. Complaining stops the flow of God in your life and releases the abilities of Satan against you.

For years instead of praying the solutions to my problems, I was praying the problem. I was putting God in a box and tying His hands. My prayers were not being heard, they hit the glass ceiling. In fact, I would dare to say that I was in bondage to my situation because of the words of my mouth. I allowed Satan to deceive me into confessing the problem repeatedly.

My head would hurt; Satan would whisper the cysts are back. I opened my mouth in fear and confessed the cysts caused my headache. Boy! was I helping Satan? On the other hand, I would confess that my husband was never going to treat me the way I thought I should be treated and he sure did not because I was confessing the problem.

Closing the Doors to Satan's Attacks: Overcoming Fear

This became a pattern for me. With each failure, I saw myself sinking in faith, fearful of the next attack and dreading the future. I did not understand that the key to effective prayer was staring me right in the face.

The Bible. That's right the Bible is your roadmap to effective prayer. Your Bible is your roadmap to ever increasing faith because faith comes by hearing and hearing by the Word of God. *So faith comes from hearing, and hearing by the word of Christ* (Romans 10:17).

Jesus said in Matthew 17:21, *"But this kind does not go out except by prayer and fasting."* There are many things in life that will require prayer to overcome. Your life should be surrounded by prayer. Prayer **MUST** become a lifestyle. If it is not, then I pray that this book will change that. Prayer unlocks the effectiveness of your armor in Ephesians 6 and releases power into your life. *And pray in the Spirit on all occasions with all kinds of prayers and requests. With this in mind, be alert and always keep on praying for all the saints* (Ephesians 6:18).

Closing the Doors to Satan's Attacks: Overcoming Fear

 **Reflection:** Get a tape recorder and keep it handy. The next time you are alone praying turn the tape recorder on and place it at a distance. This will keep you from being distracted by it. Begin your prayer time. Later play back the tape and listen to determine if you are praying or complaining. Also, listen for repetition, begging or murmuring. Ask the Lord to speak to your heart regarding your prayer life.

Though an host should encamp against me, my heart shall not fear: though war should rise against me, in this will I be confident.
Ps 27:3

Closing the Doors to Satan's Attacks: Overcoming Fear

Chapter 3
Did You Know Your Were Complaining?
Study Guide

1. One of the worst enemies of your prayer life is a complaining spirit. What does complaining do to your spiritual life?

   _____
   _____
   _____
   _____
   _____
   _____
   _____
   _____
   _____
   _____
   _____
   _____
   _____
   _____

2. What is your roadmap to effective prayer? And why?

Closing the Doors to Satan's Attacks: Overcoming Fear

3. What did your exercise with the tape recorder teach you about your prayer life?

Closing the Doors to Satan's Attacks: Overcoming Fear

4. What if anything are you going to do to make your prayer life more effective?

_____
_____
_____
_____
_____
_____
_____
_____
_____
_____
_____
_____
_____
_____
_____
_____

Chapter 4
I Didn't Know I was Complaining

For years, I would get on my knees and tell God all my problems. I would start with everything that bothered me, move to everyone that hurt me and then ask for vindication. I would complain about my finances, my marriage, and my business - in short I complained.

If I was not complaining, I was praying the problem. I am the first one to confess that nothing positive happened for me during those years in the *wilderness of complaints*. In fact, I realize now that I was tying God's hands and hindering the flow of God in my life.

There is a point in time when we must come clean if we are going to be set free. Besides, God might want to use your testimony to help someone. This is my moment in time. I was not happy and I blamed God for the mess in my life. I blamed Him for my poor health, lousy finances, messy marriage and dwindling business. Surely, I could

Closing the Doors to Satan's Attacks: Overcoming Fear

not have caused all this mess on my own. Could I? Hum. I was a walking, talking poster child for a life on the wrong road. I prayed on the wrong road for so long that I did not know that I was even on the wrong road. Until the Lord in His loving kindness showed me - ME. I finally saw a murmuring, complaining woman that was unhappy about life and yet refused to do anything about it. I desired the fullness of God, but did not know how to attain it. I attended church weekly and yet there was no effective change in my life. The problem: I did not know how to pray. The solution: Shut up and let God do the talking.

Even as the Lord was beginning to birth ministry through me, I was still learning to pray effectively, guarding my tongue with each prayer. I did not know what to pray, but once I received the Baptism of the Holy Spirit, I began to pray in my prayer language. Thereby releasing my tongue from speaking negativity into my life. *In the same way the Spirit also helps our weakness; for we do not know how to pray as we should, but the Spirit Himself intercedes for us with groanings too deep for words; and He who searches*

Closing the Doors to Satan's Attacks: Overcoming Fear

the hearts knows what the mind of the Spirit is, because He intercedes for the saints according to the will of God (Romans 8:26-27).

Complaining is a much easier release for some people and they would rather complain about a situation than seek a solution. It has become much easier for me to recognize a complainer and even easier for me to stop them in love and show them the door for an effective prayer life.

One Thursday night our Encountering God Prayer Service was discussing prayer and a woman was giving her witness about a matter, when very gently the Spirit said, *"She is complaining."* She was not asking for prayer, seeking a solution or even looking for wise counsel - she only complained.

There are times when individuals want you to join in on the pity party. Pity parties negate the power of God in your life. That old saying, "misery loves company" I believe it. Even in an atmosphere of prayer, be very

Closing the Doors to Satan's Attacks: Overcoming Fear

careful that the enemy does not creep in with murmuring and complaining and try to stop the flow of God in the prayer group. The enemy is like that, you know.

For anyone in ministry, please take this piece of advice for witnessing and counseling. Do not allow anyone to murmur and complain because it will begin to pull on your spirit. Murmuring and complaining will drain the spiritual life out of you. The individual will leave the counseling session refreshed and you leave drained wondering what happened. Listen to their concerns, but seek the Holy Spirit for guidance when the line is crossed over into complaining. I have been on the telephone or at the ministry with someone and the minute, they start to complain, my inner man does a gentle nudge or gives me a reminder that *"they are pulling on you."* When this happens, stop the session and begin to pray.

Bind the spirit that is attempting to take over and pull you and the person down. Effective prayer will stop Satan's manipulation dead in its tracks.

Closing the Doors to Satan's Attacks: Overcoming Fear

This also applies to family members, friends, co-workers and even the mail carrier. Never allow a complaining spirit to pull on you and stop the flow of God in your life.

Pray for the revelation from God for those who seek wise counsel from you. Pray that the Lord will guide you into all truths regarding this vitally important aspect of prayer.

Until I recognized I was complaining nothing changed in my life. However, through the power of the Holy Spirit, I learned to watch what I pray for and most importantly, to watch HOW I pray. Please pray the prayer at the end of this chapter and remember there is power in the spoken word.

The Power of Your Spoken Word

We can speak words about ourselves and others containing curses and spiritual death without realizing what we are spewing into the atmosphere.

Death and life are in the power of the tongue, and they who indulge in it shall eat the fruit of it [for death or life]. (Proverbs 18:21 AMP)

We need to practice the Word of God, speaking in love with patience and kindness in every sentence. *"Love is patient, love is kind and is not jealous; love does not brag and is not arrogant, does not act unbecomingly; it does not seek its own, is not provoked, does not take into account a wrong suffered, does not rejoice in unrighteousness, but rejoices with the truth; bears all things, believes all things, hopes all things, endures all things. Love never fails; but if there are gifts of prophecy, they will be done away; if there are tongues, they will cease; if there is knowledge, it will be done away* (1 Corinthians 13:4-8).

Closing the Doors to Satan's Attacks: Overcoming Fear

When our words are in alignment with the Word of God we have a special connection to God. Our words have the power of life and death. Loose the power and effects of any word curses you have spoken upon yourself and others, whether unbeknownst or in anger. Repent of having spoken evil words, remembering that to repent means to turn away from ever speaking such evil words again. If you have spoken negative words about your children, your finances, your health, your spouse, your life or your relationship with God - drop to your knees whether physically or spiritually and bind your children, finances, health, spouse, etc. to the Will of God and loose the power and effects of any wrong words you have spoken. The following prayer also will bind and loose the power and effects of any wrong words spoken about you or to you.

Behold, the LORD thy God hath set the land before thee: go up and possess it, as the LORD God of thy fathers hath said unto thee; fear not, neither be discouraged.

Deuteronomy 1:21

Chapter 4
I Didn't Know I was Complaining
Study Guide

> Your chapter 4 exercise is to begin praying for yourself and others. The following prayer is a prayer to break word curses spoken over you and your family. Begin praying this prayer on a regular basis. Initially, it may require praying this prayer daily. A night time prayer is an excellent way of getting it into your spirit.

Breaking Word Curses Spoken Over Yourself and Others

Heavenly Father, I (we) come to You now in the Name of my (our) Lord and Savior Jesus. Heavenly Father, I repent of the word curses I have spoken over myself and over (my child, my finances, my health, my mind, my spouse, my relationship to You). Heavenly Father, please forgive me for speaking these word curses according to 1 John 1:9, I ask You to destroy and break these word curses according to John 14:14 in Jesus Christ's Holy Name.

Closing the Doors to Satan's Attacks: Overcoming Fear

I am standing on your Word. You said You would give me the Keys to the Kingdom, that whatsoever I would bind on earth would be bound in heaven and whatsoever I would loose on earth would be loosed in heaven. In the Name of Jesus Christ, I bind my will to the Will of God and I pray you will make me constantly aware of Your will for my life. I bind my mind, _____'s mind to the mind of Christ that we will be aware of how Jesus would have us think and believe. Heavenly Father, in Jesus Name, I loose every wrong thought I have placed or others have placed in our minds. I loose every wrong thought I have placed into _____'s mind and every evil imagination that exalts itself against the knowledge of God. In the Name of Jesus, I loose the power and effects of any wrong words spoken to, about or by us. In the Name of Jesus Christ of Nazareth, I pray with thanksgiving. Amen![4]

Chapter 5
Stop Praying Your Problems

Recently, the Lord gave me a word regarding a web of fear and its ability to place us in bondage. Because we often pray our problems and not the solution, we bind God's hands to work on our behalf. Unfortunately, when we pray our problems we are often speaking a curse on our situation and further allowing the strongman access to our lives. Here are a several examples:

> **Woman:** Lord, I guess my husband is always going to be an alcoholic. He will never amount to anything. Help him Lord please help him.
> **QUESTION:** Help him do what? Be free or stay an alcoholic?

> **Man:** Father, my son is on crack cocaine and he is driving me crazy. He is a thief and I am tired of him. Can you move him out of my life?
> **QUESTION:** What about praying for deliverance?

> **Employee:** Lord, the people on my job make me do all the work. They never recognize me for all the work I do. They never give me any help and I must do all the work alone. They steal my supplies and I am tired of them picking on me.
>
> **QUESTION:** What about being grateful for having a job? Why not pray for the co-workers? How about taking the focus off self?

Instead of praying for a solution, they took their problems and spread them out on a buffet table lined with murmuring and complaining.

In Psalm 78:41, the people repeatedly tempted God, and pained the Holy One of Israel. What are we saying to God when we go to Him with a grocery list of complaints? What is the message that we are sending to the enemy? I believe we are saying to God, I do not trust you to work out my problems because I do not think you really know what is going on in my life. Therefore, I am coming to you to tell you about everything I am going through.

Closing the Doors to Satan's Attacks: Overcoming Fear

On the other hand, you are telling Satan, "here I am eating from your table of evil fruit." Tasting the fruit of murmuring and complaining will eventually lead to anger, resentment, jealousy and un-forgiveness. *But I say, walk by the Spirit, and you will not carry out the desire of the flesh. For the flesh sets its desire against the Spirit, and the Spirit against the flesh; for these are in opposition to one another, so that you may not do the things that you please. But if you are led by the Spirit, you are not under the Law. Now the deeds of the flesh are evident, which are: immorality, impurity, sensuality, idolatry, sorcery, enmities, strife, jealousy, outbursts of anger, disputes, dissensions, factions, envying, drunkenness, carousing, and things like these, of which I forewarn you, just as I have forewarned you, that those who practice such things will not inherit the kingdom of God* (Galatians 5:16-21).

Ephesians 4:27 warns us to give no place to the devil. There should be no open doors, windows or cracks for the enemy. The enemy needs no grand invitation to wreak havoc in your life. A moment of murmuring, complaining

Closing the Doors to Satan's Attacks: Overcoming Fear

and telling him your problems will release satanic attacks into your life.

Wrong praying will give the enemy an open invitation to step in and take matters into his hands because you have tied God's hands by praying your problems. The enemy cannot read your mind, but he can hear your words. Out of the abundance of the heart the mouth speaks. Releasing the issues you have balled up inside is vital to your spiritual growth. What is in your heart is an issue between you and the Lord. Learn the keys to effective prayer so that you will release the power of God to work on your behalf. Pray the Psalms it is an excellent place to begin because you are praying God's Word and opening your heart to receive from Him. Close the doors to Satan's attacks through the power of effective prayer. *Be anxious for nothing, but in everything by prayer and supplication with thanksgiving let your requests be made known to God* (Phil 4:6). *The effective prayer of a righteous man can accomplish much* (James 5:16).

Chapter 5
Stop Praying the Problem
Study Guide

1. We bind God's hands when we pray the problem. Explain.

Closing the Doors to Satan's Attacks: Overcoming Fear

2. Look at the scenarios at the beginning of the chapter, pray and ask the Lord to reveal any instances when you have prayed in this manner. Write them down.

_____
_____
_____
_____
_____
_____
_____
_____
_____
_____
_____
_____
_____
_____
_____

Closing the Doors to Satan's Attacks: Overcoming Fear

3. Praying the Breaking the Word Curses Prayer over yourself and others. Pray it three times today. What does praying this prayer reveal to you?

_____
_____
_____
_____
_____
_____
_____
_____
_____
_____
_____
_____
_____
_____
_____
_____
_____
_____

Closing the Doors to Satan's Attacks: Overcoming Fear

Chapter 6
Trust got a big old BUT!

When I am afraid, I will trust in you. In God, whose word I praise, in God I trust; I will not be afraid. What can mortal man do to me? (Psalm 56:3-4)

Trust in the LORD with all your heart and lean not on your own understanding; in all your ways acknowledge him, and he will make your paths straight. Do not be wise in your own eyes; fear the LORD and shun evil. This will bring health to your body and nourishment to your bones. (Prov. 3:5-8)

I know God said I would birth a ministry - BUT!

I trust the Lord to deliver my son from drugs - BUT!

I believe God is a healer - BUT!

I know Jesus saved Pookie - BUT!

God said He would provide for my needs - BUT!

Closing the Doors to Satan's Attacks: Overcoming Fear

The Lord said He would restore my marriage - BUT!

My job is about to shut down and I prayed for a new one - BUT!

Trust got a big old BUT!

One day Jesus said to his disciples, "Let's go over to the other side of the lake." So they got into a boat and set out. As they sailed, he fell asleep. A squall came down on the lake, so that the boat was being swamped, and they were in great danger. The disciples went and woke him, saying, "Master, Master, we're going to drown!" He got up and rebuked the wind and the raging waters; the storm subsided, and all was calm. Where is your faith?" he asked his disciples. In fear and amazement they asked one another, "Who is this? He commands even the winds and the water, and they obey him" (Luke 8:23-25).

Closing the Doors to Satan's Attacks: Overcoming Fear

How often have we asked the Lord to restore, bless, heal, set free or deliver? When the physical manifestation took longer than WE thought it should, we began to doubt? As soon as a storm appears on the horizon of our lives, we start to doubt. Faith and trust go right out the window with, "I know God said, BUT!"

Fear and doubt will rear their ugly heads and you will begin to walk in their fruits, cancelling out the faith required to see the move of God. Fear and doubt release the attack of Satan into your life. Once fear, doubt, and unbelief are activated, Satan has the legal right to step in and wreak havoc in your life.

Remember, Satan knows his rights and he can and will take possession of that which belongs to him. Allowing him access to your life is an open invitation to a full scale war against you. That is why you must recognize what belongs to Satan's kingdom.

What belongs to Satan? **Fear**
What does Satan use to throw you off track? **Doubt**

Closing the Doors to Satan's Attacks: Overcoming Fear

What does Satan want to kill? **Joy**

What will Satan throw at you like the wind? **Unbelief**

What does Satan want to steal? **Peace**

What does Satan want to destroy? **Your destiny**

Look at the disciples on the boat with Jesus and you can clearly see how fear, unbelief and doubt caused them miss the move of God. *One day Jesus said to his disciples, "Let's go over to the other side of the lake."*

In this sentence, Jesus is making a statement that appears simple enough, look closer. He is giving an assurance in this statement that they will go the other side of the lake. No fear, no doubt and certainly no gray or shady areas. The bible tells us that:

> *God is not a man, that He should tell or act a lie, neither the son of man, that He should feel repentance or compunction [for what He has promised]. Has He said and shall He not do it? Or has He spoken and shall He not make it good?*

Closing the Doors to Satan's Attacks: Overcoming Fear

(Numbers 23:19) and *So shall My word be that goes forth out of My mouth: it shall not return to Me void [without producing any effect, useless], but it shall accomplish that which I please and purpose, and it shall prosper in the thing for which I sent it* (Isaiah 55:11).

"Let's go over to the other side of the lake." Hearing and believing this statement will mean nothing if you do not trust in God's Word. The disciples showed this to be true the minute the storm came - trust went overboard. The winds blew - faith blew away. Raging waters slammed the boat as the bait of Satan slammed against their heads. The words of Jesus meant absolutely nothing the minute the storm began to rage. The faith that was required to weather the storm went overboard as the water crashed into the boat. *A squall came down on the lake, so that the boat was being swamped, and they were in great danger.* When the enemy is bearing down on you, will you trust in the Lord or will your faith scatter like roaches when the lights are turned on?

Closing the Doors to Satan's Attacks: Overcoming Fear

Your ability to stand in the midst of the storm will speak volumes about the depth of your trust in the Lord. Trust is the first thing to be tested when the enemy comes in like a flood. A hole in your boat will determine the strength of your trust. If your trust is shallow, then your reaction might resemble the reaction of the disciples when faced with the raging storm.

As the storm raged, the disciples raced to the other side of the boat to awaken Jesus. ***The disciples went and woke him, saying, "Master, Master, we're going to drown!"*** In other words, *"Satan said we're going to die!"* They did not believe the original words of Jesus and it clearly showed in their statement. ***"Master, Master, we're going to drown!"*** Put another way based on the fruit of their statement. "We know you said we were going to the other side of the lake, **BUT** Satan said, "We're going to drown!"

Closing the Doors to Satan's Attacks: Overcoming Fear

Trust had a BIG OLD BUT!

Master, Master, we are perishing! AMP

Master, Master, we're going to drown!" NIV

Master, Master, we are perishing!" NASB Update

Master, master, we perish. KJV

Master, master, we perish. Darby Bible

The language or version does not matter, the meaning is still the same, *we are not going to the other side, and we are going to perish.* Perish means to die, expire, pass away, give up the ghost, and take your last breath.

The disciples did not believe the initial words of Jesus and their unbelief and lack of trust is clearly shown in the frantic tone of their cries. In other words, TRUST HAD A BIG OLD BUT! Their BUT said, "We know you say you are the Son of God, BUT can you save us? "We know you have fed the multitudes, BUT can you help a brotha' out?" "We know you healed the sick, BUT this is a really big storm." Again, trust had a big old BUT.

Closing the Doors to Satan's Attacks: Overcoming Fear

Add the following scriptures to your prayer language. I pray they will strengthen your heart to *trust in the Lord with all your heart and do not lean on your own understanding. In all your ways acknowledge Him, And He will make your paths straight* (Proverbs 3:5-6). *The God of my rock; in him will I trust: he is my shield, and the horn of my salvation, my high tower, and my refuge, my saviour; thou savest me from violence* (2 Samuel 22:3).

As for God, his way is perfect; the word of the LORD is tried: he is a buckler to all them that trust in him (2 Samuel 22:31). *O LORD my God, in thee do I put my trust: save me from all them that persecute me, and deliver me* (Psalm 7:1). *Preserve me, O God: for in thee do I put my trust* (Psalm 16:1). *Trust in him at all times; ye people, pour out your heart before him: God is a refuge for us* (Psalm 62:8). *I will say of the LORD, He is my refuge and my fortress: my God; in him will I trust* (Psalm 91:2). *But mine eyes are unto thee, O GOD the Lord: in thee is my trust; leave not my soul destitute*

Closing the Doors to Satan's Attacks: Overcoming Fear

(Psalm 141:8). *Every word of God is pure: he is a shield unto them that put their trust in him* (Proverbs 30:5). *Behold, God is my salvation; I will trust, and not be afraid: for the LORD JEHOVAH is my strength and my song; he also is become my salvation* (Isaiah 12:2). In order to close the doors to Satan's attacks we must trust in the Lord - period. No ifs, ands or BUTS. Trust in Him.

Closing the Doors to Satan's Attacks: Overcoming Fear

And David said to Solomon his son, Be strong and of good courage, and do it: fear not, nor be dismayed: for the LORD God, even my God, will be with thee; he will not fail thee, nor forsake thee, until thou hast finished all the work for the service of the house of the LORD.

1 Chronicles 28:20

Chapter 6
Trust got a big old BUT!
Study Guide

Proverbs 3:5-8 tells us:
Trust in the LORD with all your heart and lean not on your own understanding; in all your ways acknowledge him, and he will make your paths straight. Do not be wise in your own eyes; fear the LORD and shun evil. This will bring health to your body and nourishment to your bones.

1. What does this verse mean to you?

_____
_____
_____
_____
_____
_____
_____
_____
_____
_____
_____
_____

Closing the Doors to Satan's Attacks: Overcoming Fear

2. Can you recall areas in your life where trust is an issue?

_____

_____

_____

_____

_____

_____

_____

_____

_____

_____

_____

_____

_____

_____

_____

_____

Closing the Doors to Satan's Attacks: Overcoming Fear

3. Would you say that TRUST in your life has a BIG OLD BUT?

_____
_____
_____
_____
_____
_____
_____
_____
_____
_____
_____
_____
_____
_____
_____
_____
_____
_____

Closing the Doors to Satan's Attacks: Overcoming Fear

4. What elements belong to Satan's kingdom? _____

   What belongs to Satan? _____

   What does Satan use to throw you off track?
   _____

   What will Satan throw at you like a ton of bricks?
   _____

   What does Satan want to kill? _____

   What does Satan want to steal? _____

   What does Satan want to destroy? _____

5. Your ability to stand in the midst of the storm will speak volumes about the depth of your trust in the Lord. Trust is the first thing tested when the enemy comes in like a flood.

   How does this statement relate to the trials you are currently going through?
   _____
   _____
   _____
   _____

Closing the Doors to Satan's Attacks: Overcoming Fear

For God hath not given us the spirit of fear; but of power, and of love, and of a sound mind.

2Timothy 1:7

Chapter 7
Recognizing the Stumbling Blocks in Your Life

The enemy has strategically placed stumbling blocks in the path of believers to hinder our destiny. Some obstacles designed by the enemy to hinder the call of God in the lives of believers can be traced back to our youth. The assault on our destiny, health, or healing is placed in such a way that although we believe we are in a state of repentance, when in fact we are not. Because some stumbling blocks are events that happened when we were young or unsaved, we bury them so far down that, we do not see them as stumbling blocks. They do not rise to the surface very often. In fact, we often suppress the memories allowing those events to create desolate places in our lives.

When the area becomes desolate, nothing can grow in or around it. It is like a patch of grass that has been killed. The entire yard looks good with the exception of the dead patch of grass that is just lying there. The dead patch hinders the yard from becoming a perfect garden. The desolate place in the yard is now a hindrance to the beauty and overall health of the yard. Because the believer is distracted by the unsightly desolate place, he cannot give his full attention to the entire yard. The result, the yard owner becomes so focused on the dead patch that other areas in the yard are left unattended. The same with believers, when the desolate place becomes the central focus such as unbelief, we loose focus on our faith and the promises of God.

Unbelief becomes the stumbling block to our blessings from the Lord. The stumbling block may be an event that was out of our control, such as an adulterous spouse, child abuse, spousal abuse, or rape. Because we did not forgive the offender, a stumbling block was created. The stumbling block is un-forgiveness. Who hindered you?

Other times the stumbling block was created by events we encountered that left a lasting impression. Events such as

Closing the Doors to Satan's Attacks: Overcoming Fear

poverty, murder, or violence. The stumbling blocks created greed, fear or mistrust.

> *And shall say, Cast ye up, cast ye up, prepare the way, take up the stumbling block out of the way of my people* (Isaiah 57:14).

Finally, stumbling blocks are created due to a number of other factors such as:
1. Sins of our youth
2. Sins committed while we were unsaved.
3. Sins committed in ignorance.
4. Rebellion
5. Disobedience

The result, sins we committed in the past became lost in the recesses of our memory, but not lost to the eyes of God. The million-dollar question: Who did hinder you? What is hindering you?

> *Ye did run well; who did hinder you that ye should not obey the truth?* (Galatians 5:7)

Closing the Doors to Satan's Attacks: Overcoming Fear

There are times when we think we are drawing close to God, but in reality, the stumbling blocks are keeping us from entering into the fullness of God. The stumbling blocks - block us. The obstacles keep us from facing the truth about our situations.

Does this mean that the stumbling block has a stumbling block? In other words, a root cause of our denial of the truth. Could it be PRIDE?

Pride will keep you from addressing the stumbling blocks. As God grows us to be more like Him, He will begin to reveal the un-confessed sin in our lives. We should go before the Lord daily in prayer and repentance. Unfortunately, we repent of the sins of today and yesterday, even last week's sins, but what about the past sins buried in 1959, 1969, 1979 or 1989? The sins of the past are equivalent to carrying around a box of old useless stuff that should be inventoried and thrown out years ago.

Closing the Doors to Satan's Attacks: Overcoming Fear

We cannot receive from God because we do not put the box down long enough to receive our blessings. We try to stretch out a finger, but God needs clean hands and a pure heart. What is the Lord's desire?

He that hath clean hands, and a pure heart; who hath not lifted up his soul unto vanity, nor sworn deceitfully. He shall receive the blessing from the LORD, and righteousness from the God of his salvation (Psalm 24:4-5).

Until we address and overcome our stumbling blocks, they will always be there waiting to hinder the move of God in us. We cannot run a steadfast race until we seek the Lord for guidance in overcoming our stumbling blocks. Without Him, we can do nothing. *For we can do nothing against the truth, but for the truth. For we are glad, when we are weak, and ye are strong: and this also we wish, even your perfection* (2 Corinthians 13:8-9).

Closing the Doors to Satan's Attacks: Overcoming Fear

You ran well but who or what did hinder you?
- ✓ What truth did you not obey?
- ✓ What lie did you believe?
- ✓ Whose report did you receive?

Believe it or not fear can become a deadly stumbling block and your worst enemy. Pray and ask the Lord to reveal the stumbling blocks and put and end to them.

Chapter 7
Recognizing the Stumbling Blocks in Your Life
Study Guide

1. The enemy has strategically placed stumbling blocks in the path of believers to

   _____

2. Describe a desolate place.

   _____
   _____
   _____
   _____
   _____
   _____
   _____
   _____
   _____
   _____
   _____

Closing the Doors to Satan's Attacks: Overcoming Fear

_____

_____

_____

_____

3. Do you see a desolate place in your life? Explain.

_____

_____

_____

_____

_____

_____

_____

_____

_____

_____

_____

Closing the Doors to Satan's Attacks: Overcoming Fear

4. We cannot receive from God because we do not put the box down long enough to receive our blessings. We try to stretch out a finger, but God needs clean hands and a pure heart. What is the Lord's desire based on Psalm 24:4-5?

_____
_____
_____
_____
_____
_____
_____
_____
_____
_____
_____
_____
_____
_____
_____
_____

Closing the Doors to Satan's Attacks: Overcoming Fear

5. Until we address and overcome the obstacles in our lives they will always be there waiting to hinder the move of God in our lives. Explain.

_____
_____
_____
_____
_____
_____
_____
_____
_____
_____
_____
_____
_____
_____
_____

Chapter 8
Fear: The World's Deadliest Stumbling Block & Your Worst Enemy

Many visions have become the prey of fear, the world's deadliest obstacle and your worst enemy. Fear is the tool the enemy uses to stop the flow of God in the life of the believer. It is also the trap that is often set when a believer is walking into his destiny.

At times, it creeps in with a demonic subtly and other times it comes in with a demonic fury. Whatever the case, when fear comes the objective is to wage war against the people of God.

The thief (fear) comes only to steal and kill and destroy (John 10:10). Fear enters in to steal your destiny, kill you joy and destroy your faith and trust in God. Fear can completely disrupt your flow with God. Once the roots and fruits of fear set in, a domino effect occurs that creates a devastating chain reaction against you.

Closing the Doors to Satan's Attacks: Overcoming Fear

Here are a few of the fruits of fear:

- Torment
- Despair
- Moral Decay
- Destruction
- Anxiety
- Spiritual Death
- Suffering
- Disbelief
- Violence
- Depression

Fear is a tool that Satan uses to render the believer:

- Powerless
- Inadequate
- Loveless
- Weak
- Lukewarm
- Mentally Bankrupt
- Lifeless
- Ineffective
- Hopeless
- Negative or doubtful

Fear is one of Satan's most effective tools for hindering the advancement of the Kingdom of God. Because fear is so invasive, it can penetrate the inner most parts of an individuals being.

The bible tells us that, God is no respecter of persons. Allow me to drop you a nugget: Fear is no respecter of

Closing the Doors to Satan's Attacks: Overcoming Fear

persons, either. Fear is unconcerned with your race, creed or color. Fear has no boundaries, geographic preferences, denominational affiliations, economic criteria or sexual orientation. Fear is omnipresent - it is everywhere. Waiting for an opportunity to wage a full-scale demonic attack against humanity.

Understanding Fear

Unfortunately, as humans we have not been taught the relevance of understanding the origin of fear. When you understand your enemy, you are more equipped to defeat him. I must admit that it has taken years to come to grips with the fears in my life. Later in this book, I am going to share my journey into fear with you.

To understand the origin of fear let us look at the origin of man. In Genesis chapter 3:10 Adam makes this statement, *"I heard the sound of You in the garden, and I was afraid because I was naked; so I hid myself."* Did you read that? *I was afraid...* Adam's response was a response of fear.

Closing the Doors to Satan's Attacks: Overcoming Fear

Therefore, fear began with the first man, Adam and it has tormented the world ever since. Fear will cause you to hide from your destiny. It will cause you to hide from the very thing God has for you. Here are a few examples, if one of them bites you, just holler OUCH!

- ✓ God said, "Preach My Word."
    - ➢ You reply, "I'm Afraid." (Fear)
- ✓ God said, "Seek My Face."
    - ➢ You reply, "I am not ready." (Fear)
- ✓ God said, "Live Holy."
    - ➢ You keep shacking up. (Rebellion)
- ✓ God said, "Go to college."
    - ➢ You reply, "I can't afford it." (Doubt)
- ✓ God said, "Wait on Me."
    - ➢ You reply, "God is not blessing me." (Doubt)

What Causes Fear

Now that you know the origin of fear, it is now time to recognize what causes fear. A more appropriate statement would be who causes fear?

Closing the Doors to Satan's Attacks: Overcoming Fear

Satan - Although Satan has an arsenal of weapons to use against humanity, fear is one of his strongest weapons against us. He uses fear the way a swordsman uses a sword, swift and with demonic precision. He knows just where to strike - right at the heart of fear.

Evil Spirits - Satan's army of demonic spirits are dispatched against us to bring about fear in every area of our life. They also wield the weapon of fear with great precision because it is their ultimate assignment to tear down the people of God.

The Media - I remember saying to my husband one evening while watching television, "television is the propaganda machine to instill fear into the hearts of individuals." Try watching the news every night for years, they spew doom and gloom like running water. The good things happening in the world receive a small sound bite, while every tragedy around the world is sensationalized night after night.

Closing the Doors to Satan's Attacks: Overcoming Fear

Religion - Please do not hate me for this one, but religion in the wrong hands is a dangerous thing. People are dying everyday in the name of religion. Religious zealot's spew hatred, murder, discord and fear all in the name of religion. They never mention love in their speeches or rhetoric; they spew anger, prejudice and resentment while crying out for justice. The only justice they will receive is at the hand of the Almighty God. They have a form of religion but they do not have a relationship with El Shaddai. They do not know Jesus and often do not acknowledge Him as the Son of God. Finally, they are not led by the Holy Spirit of God. What spirit is leading them?

> *"By myself I have sworn, my mouth has uttered in all integrity a word that will not be revoked: Before me every knee will bow; by me every tongue will swear. They will say of me, 'In the LORD alone are righteousness and strength.'" All who have raged against him will come to him and be put to shame* (Isaiah 45:23-24).

Closing the Doors to Satan's Attacks: Overcoming Fear

It is written: "'As surely as I live,' says the Lord, 'every knee will bow before me; every tongue will confess to God'" (Romans 14:11).

...that at the name of Jesus every knee should bow, in heaven and on earth and under the earth, and every tongue confess that Jesus Christ is Lord (Philippians 2:10-11).

People - People can be an integral part of instilling fear into our lives. Parents can instill fear in their children, spouses instill fear into their mates, children instill fear into other children and the list goes on. If you are spoon fed fear on a daily basic, fear is the only thing you will recognize. It is sad to say, but humanity is the worst proponent in the spread of fear. People that walk in fear spread fear. Some of the most outwardly confident people are the most inwardly fearful people in the world.

Pay close attention to a loud, need to be the life of the party individual, you will often find a person that lacks

Closing the Doors to Satan's Attacks: Overcoming Fear

self-confidence, and needs constant validation from others. When these elements are combined, you will discover an individual that thrives on demeaning others with fear, ridicule and intimidation. Their sole purpose is to keep others from recognizing the fear that dwells within them.

How does Fear Attack
Fear can attack an individual in several ways:
* The Physical Attack
* The Mental Attack
* The Spiritual Attack

Any one of the above stated attacks can be devastating to the believer. If left unchecked the enemy will kill, steal and destroy by using one or all of these elements in the attack.

The Physical Attack:
Your body is the place he will strike beginning with a small pain and leading to a bad diagnosis from the doctor.

Closing the Doors to Satan's Attacks: Overcoming Fear

I believe the enemy enjoys the physical attack because there are so many areas in the body to choose.

The Lord has healed me eight times and with each illness, the enemy came at me with full guns blazing. He attacked my head with cysts, which resulted in four surgeries; I was diagnosed with macular degeneration, I developed pains in my arm and heart; a large tumor was removed from my breast; and I developed high blood pressure. With each attack, the Lord healed me completely. *Heal me, O LORD, and I will be healed; save me and I will be saved, for you are the one I praise* (Jeremiah 17:14).

The Mental Attack:

The mind is the **battleground** of the devil. To phrase it another way: the mind is the **playground** of the devil. If you do not have the Word of God on your mind, the enemy will launch an all out strike against your mind. If he can control the mind, the rest of your life will follow.

Closing the Doors to Satan's Attacks: Overcoming Fear

Let this mind be in you, which was also in Christ Jesus (Philippians 2:5). Keep the Lord at the forefront of your heart and mind and he will keep you in perfect peace. *Thou wilt keep him in perfect peace, whose mind is stayed on thee: because he trusteth in thee* (Isaiah 26:3).

The Spiritual Attack:

This is where the rubber meets the road. The enemy will do everything in his limited power to keep you out of God's presence.

★ Satan does not care if you go to church - *just don't praise God.*
★ He is not concerned if you pray - *just don't trust God.*
★ He is not concerned if you carry a bible - *don't believe the Word of God.*

The spiritual attack is designed to assassinate your faith and trust in God. If the enemy can kill your faith in God your entire life will seem hopeless and lost. A weak prayer life is an inroad to an all out spiritual attack. It is vital that we guard our heart and mind. *And the peace of*

Closing the Doors to Satan's Attacks: Overcoming Fear

God, which transcends all understanding, will guard your hearts and your minds in Christ Jesus (Philippians 4:7).

Throughout the years, the Lord has done great things in my life. With each miracle or promise, my faith has continued to increase. During my most recent twenty-one consecration, the Lord said that as I walked out of the consecration I would walk out with clarity of purpose.

Silly me, I thought I would walk through the consecration and come out with a new and exciting revelation of my purpose and destiny. I had no idea that the day the consecration ended, I would be faced with an attack by the enemy unlike any other in my 40+ years of living. The Lord told me during the consecration that I would encounter a storm, but not to worry, He would be with me.

I was reminded of Jesus being tempted by the devil when he was in the desert fasting for forty days.

Closing the Doors to Satan's Attacks: Overcoming Fear

*Jesus, full of the Holy Spirit, returned from the Jordan and was led by the Spirit in the desert, where for forty days he was **tempted by the devil**. He ate nothing during those days, and at the end of them, he was hungry* (Luke 4:1-2).

Knowing that the Lord would be with me as I went through the storm proved to be a great comfort. For me He was Jehovah Shammah (The Lord is There).

To begin with, the enemy attacked my health by disturbing the nerve in my head. The result, very painful headaches. If that was not enough, I experienced pains in my chest. While battling the headaches, I was slowly being attacked by fear. The fear developed because I failed to walk through several doors the Lord opened for me. The Lord began to deal with me regarding the fear and each time I went before the Lord, He reminded me of assignments I left incomplete, in other words, doors left open for Satan's attacks.

Closing the Doors to Satan's Attacks: Overcoming Fear

There was a piece of property the Lord instructed me to possess. Fear kept me from making the necessary telephone calls. Fear kept me from praying about the property. In fact, I would avoid the property all together.

One morning while in prayer I began to pray Psalm 27 and the Lord stopped me dead in my tracks. I prayed:

The LORD is my light and my salvation— whom shall I fear? The LORD is the stronghold of my life—of whom shall I be afraid? When evil men advance against me to devour my flesh, when my enemies and my foes attack me, they will stumble and fall. Though an army besiege me, my heart will not fear (Psalm 27:1-3).

As I prayed the verse, *"my heart will not fear"* the Spirit of the Lord said, *"stop right there."* He went on to say, *"read it again."* I began to read again and when I got to the verse, *"my heart will not fear"* the Holy Spirit said, *"that's not true, you are walking in fear."*

Closing the Doors to Satan's Attacks: Overcoming Fear

I sat on the couch in shock. You could have bought me for a food stamp. The Spirit of the Lord then said, *"you did not call the woman about the building."* I began to repent and ask the Lord's forgiveness, but that was not what He wanted. Repenting did not take the fear away. Acting on His directive is what moves fear out of the way and binds the enemy. I picked up the telephone and called the realtor. After leaving a message with the secretary, I went back to prayer and once again I ask the Lord to forgive me. Never again will I walk in fear; *God did not give me the spirit of fear; but of power, and of love, and of a sound mind* (2 Timothy 1:7).

I now realize the reason I walked in fear, simply stated the vision appeared too big for me. My mind could not grasp the vastness of the destiny the Lord set before me and the only thing I could see was the tremendous giant in the form of the building. Fear had such a grip on me that I was willing to miss God in order to avoid facing the giant. I did not practice what I preached. I have always said, *where God gives a vision, He will give provision.*

Closing the Doors to Satan's Attacks: Overcoming Fear

The Lord has a purpose and plan for our lives and as long as we are in the center of His will, He will open every door to accomplish His plan. If we allow fear to creep in, the enemy will infiltrate the plan and hinder the move of God.

It is my prayer that you will seek the Lord for any remnants or residue of fear that could be waiting to rob you of your destiny. You must bind the strongman if you are to walk into the fullness of your destiny. Whenever fear is revealed immediately go into action. Write out a plan for conquering fear. The best way to conquer fear is to develop a strategy for addressing fear at its root cause. A strategic plan is necessary for overcoming fear and living a victorious life. Make sure your plan begins and ends with prayer.

>...*fear was on every side* (Psalm 31:13)...*But I trusted in thee, O LORD: I said, Thou art my God* (Psalm 31:14).

After these things the word of the LORD came unto Abram in a vision, saying, **Fear not***, Abram: I am thy shield, and* *thy exceeding great reward.*

Genesis 15:1

Chapter 8
Fear: The World's Deadliest Stumbling Block & Your Worst Enemy
Study Guide

1. Many destinies have become the prey of fear, the world's deadliest obstacle and _____.

2. Fear is the tool the enemy uses to stop the flow of God in the life of the believer. It is also the trap that is often set when a believer is walking into his destiny.
   True or False

3. Write out several examples of the fruits of fear
   _____
   _____
   _____
   _____
   _____
   _____
   _____

Closing the Doors to Satan's Attacks: Overcoming Fear

Closing the Doors to Satan's Attacks: Overcoming Fear

4. Fear is a tool that Satan uses to render the believer:

Closing the Doors to Satan's Attacks: Overcoming Fear

5. Describe the following attacks against the believer:

Fear can attack an individual in several ways:

* The Physical Attack

_____
_____
_____
_____
_____
_____
_____
_____
_____
_____
_____
_____
_____
_____
_____
_____

Closing the Doors to Satan's Attacks: Overcoming Fear

* The Mental Attack

Closing the Doors to Satan's Attacks: Overcoming Fear

* The Spiritual Attack

Chapter 9
FEAR NOT!

There are times in every person's life when we must deal with fear. Like it or not fear will find a way to creep its ugly little head into our lives. Always at a moment when we are at a pivotal point of going through or breaking out. Few of us understand fear and being acquainted with fear is not a comfortable idea. We can fear new things such as a new job, new surroundings and new people in our lives. We fear medical procedures, death, the trauma of divorce, the agony of defeat, school exams and the list goes on. When you think about fear as a whole, fear is one of those things in life that refuses to be pampered, coddled, diverted or patronized. Fear will find a little crack in your foundation and slither its way in. Once fear enters in it will take over.

When fear enters your life this is the time to fall face down before the Lord and cry out to Him to for mercy. *Let us therefore come boldly unto the throne of grace, that*

Closing the Doors to Satan's Attacks: Overcoming Fear

we may obtain mercy, and find grace to help in time of need (Hebrews 4:16).

When you bring fear to the feet of Jesus - what can you expect in return? There are several things you can expect when you turn your situation over to the Lord. You can expect:

1. **The strength of His presence.**

    Remember in First Samuel when David was returning to his camp to find Ziklag had been raided and all the women and children were captured including his wives. David and his men wept. Later the men wanted to kill David.

    First Samuel 30:6 says that, "And David was greatly distressed; for the people spake of stoning him, because the soul of all the people was grieved, every man for his sons and for his daughters: but David encouraged himself in the LORD his God.

Closing the Doors to Satan's Attacks: Overcoming Fear

Nevertheless, he took his fear into the presence of the Lord. David crawled to the Lord in profound weakness. The moment he lifted his empty hands to heaven and grabbed a double portion of the Lord His God, strength hit his system like a shot of lightning. Now think about this, his circumstances did not change - David changed. David experienced God's strength and he found a way to put that strength to work.

2. **Perspective in His presence**

In God's strength David was able to gain, perspective on the situation and David asked for clear direction from the Lord and clear direction is what he received. Once you have found strength in the Lord, ask Him for His will in your situation. He will direct your path when you turn the path over to Him.

3. **The Fragrance of His presence**

Once you have cried out to the Lord and found refuge in Him, you are able to fall into His arms in a way that is beyond anything you will ever experience. The *fragrance of His presence* will leave an everlasting impression in your life. You will forever be changed.

4. **Insight in His presence**

    When we bring our fears to the Lord, we receive strength, perspective, and a whiff of His refreshing presence. More than that, we gain *insight into His presence* through deeper insights into God's Word and nature.

5. **A lasting memory of His presence**

    After we have run to the Lord with our fears, instead of allowing us to become paralyzed or traumatized, He gives us something to point to or better still a monument to reflect on for the rest of our days. If there had been no fearful tragedy in your life, there would have been no mighty deliverance, no monument or pointer and no lasting memory of His help. There would be no monument of God's power and grace during the darkest period of our lives.

Closing the Doors to Satan's Attacks: Overcoming Fear

Know this:
1. No matter what we might be facing at the time.
2. No matter how crazy the odds against us.
3. No matter how black the sky looks.
4. No matter how big the giants we are facing.

We will look back and say, do you see! Do you remember how bad it was? People said there was no hope, no help, no healing. The Philistines were upon us! But Almighty God, *El Shaddai,* showed up and in His fearsome presence we found a hiding place of strength, perspective, fragrance and insight.

The LORD is my light and my salvation; whom shall I fear? the LORD is the strength of my life; of whom shall I be afraid? When the wicked, even mine enemies and my foes, came upon me to eat up my flesh, they stumbled and fell. Though an host should encamp against me, my heart shall not fear (Psalm 27:1-3). FEAR NOT! The Lord is with you.

Closing the Doors to Satan's Attacks: Overcoming Fear

Take a look at a list of strategies for overcoming fear. Please keep in mind that you won't find a cookie cutter, ready made, microwave solution, but I pray that the steps outlined will be the beginning of your journey of overcoming fear.

You will find a prayer at the end of chapter ten for binding the spirit of fear that is over shadowing your life.

Closing the Doors to Satan's Attacks: Overcoming Fear

Strategy for Overcoming Fear

Here is an outline to help address the fear in your life.

1. Write out the plans God has spoken over the years.
2. Make a list of the steps you have taken to accomplish His plans.
3. Make a list of things you did not complete.
4. Search your heart for the reasons you failed to follow His instructions.
5. Read Second Timothy 1:7 daily.
6. Ask the Lord for strength to walk out His plans.
7. Make a list of the things in your life that cause fear.
8. Daily read the scriptures on the next page and continue to add to the list. Study to show yourself approved unto God…
9. Purpose in your heart; never give place to the devil by allowing him to steal your destiny. If God called you to it, He will see you through it.
10. Begin to bind the strongman through prayer whenever he rears his ugly head. Never give place to the devil. (See the Prayer for binding the Strongman Prayer).

Closing the Doors to Satan's Attacks: Overcoming Fear

Chapter 9
FEAR NOT!
Study Guide

1. When you bring fear to the feet of Jesus - what can you expect in return? There are several things you can expect when you turn your situation over to the Lord. What can you expect?

_____

_____

_____

_____

_____

_____

_____

_____

_____

_____

_____

Closing the Doors to Satan's Attacks: Overcoming Fear

Closing the Doors to Satan's Attacks: Overcoming Fear

2. Look at a list of strategies for overcoming fear. How can you apply these strategies to your life?

_____
_____
_____
_____
_____
_____
_____
_____
_____
_____
_____
_____
_____
_____
_____
_____
_____
_____

Closing the Doors to Satan's Attacks: Overcoming Fear

Chapter 10
Taking Back Your God Given Authority: Binding the Strongman in Your Life

How many of us have had things manipulated from us by Satan? Have you ever felt slain by the giants in your life? More regrettably is how many of us handed over our destiny to Satan? When we walk in his evil steps he has legal rights to come against us. He has the legal right to steal from us. He came to kill, steal, and destroy your destiny.

Things you handed over to the enemy:
* Peace   * Love   * Joy   * Home
* Money   * Job\career   * Health   * Children
* Self-esteem   * Ministry   * Marriage   * Business
* Sexual purity

Take heart, God promises to give you back double what you lost. *Fear not, O land; be glad and rejoice: for the LORD will do great things* (Joel 2:21). God will restore that which belongs to us. But before He does, He requires us to confront our problems with a holy determination - a state of mind that first leans on God, draws strength from Him, and then says, "I am never giving up." The Lord said in Psalm 84:11, *no good thing will he withhold from them that walk uprightly.* We must begin to walk in the authority given to us by Christ Jesus.

Instead of their shame my people will receive a double portion, and instead of disgrace they will rejoice in their inheritance; and so they will inherit a double portion in their land, and everlasting joy will be theirs (Isaiah 61:7).

The LORD will grant that the enemies who rise up against you will be defeated before you. They will come at you from one direction but flee from you in seven. The LORD will send a blessing on your barns and on everything you put your hand to. The LORD your God will bless you in the land he is giving you. The LORD will establish you as his holy

Closing the Doors to Satan's Attacks: Overcoming Fear

people, as he promised you on oath, if you keep the commands of the LORD your God and walk in his ways (Deuteronomy 28:7).

I will repay you for the years the locusts have eaten—the great locust and the young locust, the other locusts and the locust swarm—my great army that I sent among you. You will have plenty to eat, until you are full, and you will praise the name of the LORD your God, who has worked wonders for you; never again will my people be shamed (Joel 2:25-26).

For when God made the promise to Abraham, since He could swear by no one greater, He swore by Himself, saying, "I WILL SURELY BLESS YOU AND I WILL SURELY MULTIPLY YOU." And so, having patiently waited, he obtained the promise (Hebrews 6:10-13).

Closing the Doors to Satan's Attacks: Overcoming Fear

See, I set before you today life and prosperity, death and destruction. For I command you today to love the LORD your God, to walk in his ways, and to keep his commands, decrees and laws; then you will live and increase, and the LORD your God will bless you in the land you are entering to possess (Deuteronomy 30:15-16).

The choice is yours: You can pray about the situation or you can complain about the situation. Remember, you do have a choice. BE NOT DECEIVED! Satan is out to kill, steal and destroy your life. Do not waste another day leaving a door open for him to walk in and steal from you.

Binding the Strongman:

While writing this book, the Lord spoke this word through Dr. Margaret Wright regarding the enemy's attack against me. The Lord said, *"You could not have had this walk of faith until you bound and destroyed the strong man which was fear. When you bind the strongman, you are binding fear. Then you release God's hands to move on your*

Closing the Doors to Satan's Attacks: Overcoming Fear

behalf. Until then you are a slave to the strongman and you are in his grips and God can't touch you. Satan has a license when you walk in fear.

Once you are released and set free, God can legally work for you. As long as you are under the influence of the strongman, he can legally come against you. Once you bind the strongman and release God's will into your life, you have opened a legal door for God to move on your behalf. "I stand at the door and knock..." God put one element in man that He won't go over - man's will. The will must be surrendered. When we say, "I need help." I have to decided, "No more fear." "I will allow God to help me."

We must bind the strongman that is trying to come against us. We must take authority in the Name of Jesus.

*He called his twelve disciples to him and gave them **authority** to drive out evil spirits and to heal every disease and sickness (Matthew 10:1).*

Closing the Doors to Satan's Attacks: Overcoming Fear

*Then Jesus came to them and said, "**All authority** in heaven and on earth has been given to me. Therefore go and make disciples of all nations, baptizing them in the name of the Father and of the Son and of the Holy Spirit, and teaching them to obey everything I have commanded you. And surely I am with you always, to the very end of the age"* (Matthew 28:18-20).

*I will give you the keys of the kingdom of heaven; whatever you **bind on earth** will be **bound in heaven**, and whatever you loose on earth will be loosed in heaven"* (Matthew 16:19).

Chapter 10
Taking Back Your God Given Authority: Binding the Strongman in Your Life
Study Guide

Your assignment for this chapter is to pray the Disabling Strongmen Prayer below. Pray the prayer first thing in the morning and before you go to bed at night. Remember, prayer is the key that changes things.

Disabling Strongmen Prayer

Heavenly Father, I come to You in the Name of my Lord and Savior Christ Jesus. Holy Spirit I pray that You will quicken me to hear my Heavenly Father's Voice and to lead me in prayer. Heavenly Father, I bow down and worship before You. I come to You with praise and with thanksgiving. I come to you in humility, in fear, in trembling and seeking truth. I come to You in gratitude, in love, and through the precious Blood of Your Son Jesus Christ of Nazareth.

Closing the Doors to Satan's Attacks: Overcoming Fear

Strongman called spirit of rejection, spirit of anti-Christ, spirit of error, spirit of seducing spirit, spirit of bondage, spirit of death, spirit of divination, spirit of dumb and deaf, spirit of familiar spirit, spirit of fear, spirit of pride, spirit of Leviathan, spirit of heaviness, spirit of infirmity, spirit of jealousy, spirit of lying, spirit of perverse spirit, and spirit of whoredom; I rebuke you and bind you in the Name of the Lord Jesus Christ, along with all your works, roots, fruits, tentacles, links, that are in my presence, the presence of anybody I prayed for today, every organ, every cell, every gland, every muscle, every ligament, every bone in our bodies, our houses, cars, trucks, buildings, properties, and pets, and I loose you to go where Jesus Christ sends you. I apply the Blood of Jesus over myself, each person I prayed for today, our houses, cars, properties, offices, and work places and pets as our protection.

Lord Jesus, I ask You to destroy any familiar spirit that has allowed any of these demonic strongmen into our presence. In the Name of the Lord Jesus Christ according to John 14:14.

Closing the Doors to Satan's Attacks: Overcoming Fear

Heavenly Father, I ask You to loose into each of us: the Spirit of Adoption (Romans 8:15), the Spirit of Truth (1 John 4:6, Psalm 51:10), the Holy Spirit of Truth (John 16:13), the Spirit of Resurrection Life and life more Abundantly (John 11:25), John 10:10b), the Holy Spirit and His Gifts (1 Corinthians 12:9-12). In the Name of Jesus. Amen.

And Moses said unto the people, Fear ye not, stand still, and see the salvation of the LORD, which he will show to you today: for the Egyptians whom ye have seen today, ye shall see them again no more for ever.
Exodus 14:13

Chapter 11
Is There Residue From Your Past?

Is there residue from your past that still haunts your future? The Lord spoke to me regarding the residue of my past. He warned me to resolve any residue hindering my destiny.

As we begin to cleanse our spiritual homes we must be aware of the residue of un-confessed sins, incomplete assignments, strongholds or generational curses that still exists. They will eventually become a stumbling block to your destiny.

We cannot close the door to Satan's attacks if we have un-resolved issues or residue from the past. We must not leave desolate places for Satan's infiltration. The residue of the past can contribute to miscarriages of our destiny. I use the word miscarriage because birthing your destiny is the equivalent of birthing a child.

Closing the Doors to Satan's Attacks: Overcoming Fear

No mother wants her baby miscarried or stillborn. The pain and anguish the mother must endure as she deals with the revelation that her child does not have the breath of life. Our spiritual birthing process is similar to the natural birthing process.

See for yourself.
- The child is conceived in the womb.
- The destiny is conceived in the spiritual womb.

- The child is carried by the mother.
- The vision is carried by the believer.

- The child reaches term and ready to come into the world.
- The vision reaches the season when God is ready to release you.

- The labor pains begin.
- The attacks [pains] come from the enemy.

Closing the Doors to Satan's Attacks: Overcoming Fear

- The mother's water breaks.
- The believer sheds sweat and tears as he presses for the mark of his destiny.

WAIT!!
What happens if fear sets in?

Unlike the natural birth mother who cannot help but push the believer can stop pressing. The test comes at the moment the destiny is in the spiritual birth canal. What happens when:

- Fear sets in - **the believer stops pushing**.
- Doubt raises its head - **the believer stops pushing**.
- A negative report is received - **the believer stops pushing.**

The list could continue for another sixty-pages, but I pray you get the idea. Each example became a stronghold and stopped the move of God. In other words, the destiny was miscarried.

Closing the Doors to Satan's Attacks: Overcoming Fear

It is vital to the destiny set before us that we address the residue of the past. *"Search me, O Lord, Search me and know my heart…"*

For almost a year, I walked in fear that started with a building. The building became my giant and I almost miscarried the vision because of fear. The door to fear was opened in 2007 and remained opened until July 2008.

Fear of the building gave Satan an open invitation to drop seeds of fear in other areas along the way. The result, the move of God was hindered because of the desolate place in my heart. Fear created a desolate place where faith could not grow.

It is important to understand that closing the doors to Satan's attacks is essential to our spiritual health. Anything left on the "spiritual books" can be on open invitation for his attacks. I left the door open for fear to come in, which in turned allowed Satan's attack to come against me.

Closing the Doors to Satan's Attacks: Overcoming Fear

I began my spiritual inventory with Psalm 139; then moving to Psalm 51 and finally Psalm 61.

This might seem overwhelming to you but please pray Psalm 61 because in it you will find comfort:

> *Hear my cry, O God; attend unto my prayer. From the end of the earth will I cry unto thee, when my heart is overwhelmed: lead me to the rock that is higher than I. For thou hast been a shelter for me, and a strong tower from the enemy. I will abide in thy tabernacle for ever: I will trust in the covert of thy wings. Selah* (Psalm 61:1-4).

I decided that nothing would separate me from all that the Lord has for me. Nothing from the past, present or future will keep me from the plans the Lord has for me. In order to press forward, you must make a similar decision.

Closing the Doors to Satan's Attacks: Overcoming Fear

What happens when we are in a hurry to give birth to the vision?

Unfortunately, many people are trying to give birth too soon. The natural child requires nine months, but what would happen if the mother decided to give birth in two months. The baby would be born premature and in some cases stillborn.

It is the same with the spiritual birth, the individual is so hungry for ministry, business, leadership or career that they pre-maturely give birth to the vision. They launch out before the appointed time by God and miss the vital impartation of wisdom He desires for them. We must wait on the Lord to give us clear directions. Clear direction is accomplished through several means:
1. His Word
2. His Voice
3. Wise Counsel

Closing the Doors to Satan's Attacks: Overcoming Fear

Reflection: *Somewhere along the journey of fulfilling the great commission, individuals began thinking that ministry was glamorous and the determination to "make it happen" superseded the voice of the Lord. Thereby causing them to launch out too soon. For the poor misguided souls that think TRUE ministry is glamorous, please allow me to clarify for you. TRUE ministry is NOT what you see on television or hear on the radio - so don't believe the hype.*

The Lord said in Jeremiah 29:11: *For I know the plans I have for you," declares the LORD, "plans to prosper you and not to harm you, plans to give you hope and a future.*

He also told us in Habakkuk 2:2-3: *And the LORD answered me, and said, Write the vision, and make it plain upon tables, that he may run that readeth it. For the vision is yet for an appointed time, but at the end it shall speak, and not lie: though it tarry, wait for it; because it will surely come, it will not tarry* (KJV).

Closing the Doors to Satan's Attacks: Overcoming Fear

Finally in Isaiah 40:31: *But they that wait upon the LORD shall renew their strength; they shall mount up with wings as eagles; they shall run, and not be weary; and they shall walk, and not faint* (KJV).

Even when the **WAIT** and the **WEIGHT** seem to last forever He said in Galatians 6:9, *And let us not be weary in well doing: for in due season we shall reap, if we faint not.*

Speaking of your due season, I recommend an audio series entitled, *"Recognizing Your Due Season."* I am sure that it will bless you as you walk into your due season. Please visit my website for more information.

In order to walk into our due season we must seek the Lord for guidance because He will lead and guide you into all truth. Jesus answered in John 14:6, *"I am the way and the truth and the life. No one comes to the Father except through me.*

Closing the Doors to Satan's Attacks: Overcoming Fear

I believe the first place He will lead us is to a place of repentance. Through repentance the Lord can begin to deal with us about our open doors and desolate places. The repentant heart is the place where God will begin to clean out the fragments and debris. He will clean out the residue that keeps you from the purpose and plan He has for you.

We must address the residue if we are to move forward. Are you ready to move forward?

Closing the Doors to Satan's Attacks: Overcoming Fear

Chapter 11
Is There Residue From Your Past?
Study Guide

Your assignment in this chapter is to perform the following:

1. Go before the Lord in prayer.
2. Ask Him to reveal un-confessed sins that are hindering your growth.
3. Read the following verses and add them to your prayers.
4. Repent of every issue the Lord brings to your heart.
5. When you go before the Lord make sure you have a pen and paper.

The Repentant Heart

When we go before the Lord we must go with a repentant heart. *The sacrifices of God are a broken spirit; a broken and contrite heart, O God, you will not despise* (Psalm 51:17). *For this is what the high and lofty One says—he who lives forever, whose name is holy: "I live in a high and holy place, but also with him who is contrite and lowly in spirit, to revive the spirit of the lowly and to revive the heart of the contrite* (Isaiah 57:15).

Closing the Doors to Satan's Attacks: Overcoming Fear

In order for our prayers to be heard we must have a contrite or repentant heart. The Lord inhabits the praises of His people, but only if we have a repentant heart. Therefore, we must go boldly before the throne of grace in true repentance, seeking the face of God and not the hand of God.

Let us then fearlessly, confidently, and boldly draw near to the throne of grace (the throne of God's unmerited favor to us sinners), that we may receive mercy [for our failures] and find grace to help in good time for every need [appropriate help and well-timed help, coming just when we need it] (Hebrews 4:16).

Chapter 12
My Journey of Overcoming Fear

We have all had our share of life's journey of trials and tribulations, if you have not - keep on living because you will. The trials and tribulations we have faced were strategically designed to shape us into the people we are today. Whether we allowed the issues from our past to grow us or to destroy us, we did have a choice.

Think about children who grew up as orphans. Did the fact that they grew up without parents make them stronger or make them bitter? What about children who grew up in abusive homes? It does not matter whether the abuse was physical, sexual or mental - abuse is still abuse. Did the abuse from the past determine the depth of growth in the person or like so many others, did the abuse lie dormant shaping the person into a bitter, fearful, rebellious adult? Did any of these events birth a rebellious heart against God or society to the extent that trust did not exist in their vocabulary?

Closing the Doors to Satan's Attacks: Overcoming Fear

Our past is a tool that will shape our future. It is up to us to decide to choose sides. Are we on the side of the line that says, *"I grew up used and abused, therefore I don't trust people and I don't trust God."* Are we on the side of the line that says, *"What Satan meant for bad, God has used it for my good?" I am not going to allow the pains from my past to destroy my future. I trust God and I know that my trials will be the very testimony that helps someone else. I will not be ashamed because I am more than a conqueror. I am an over comer by the blood of the Lamb and by the very words of my testimony. My testimony is a sure foundation through Christ Jesus."*

There are days when we want to give up and walk away. There are days when fear wants to be our best friend. Days when we want to stay in bed, pull the covers up, and never come out again. How would God get the glory if we allowed any of these things to happen? Satan would get the glory and he who wins the victory gets the glory.

Closing the Doors to Satan's Attacks: Overcoming Fear

My life of adversity was shaped when I was a child. Both my parents were deceased by the time I was 15 years of age and if Satan had his way I would have been dead by the time I was 16. Because of the trauma of losing my parents, I was often lonely, afraid and at one point in my young life, suicidal. I can now look back at my past and see how God used each event to shape me into the woman I have become. Even though the pain and trauma of my past was dormant for many years, God in His infinite wisdom began to reveal the heartaches in such a way that I could deal with each tragedy and come out an over comer.

I understand as the Apostle Paul wrote in Philippians 4:12, *I know both how to be abased, and I know how to abound: everywhere and in all things I am instructed both to be full and to be hungry, both to abound and to suffer need.* Through the trials and tribulations of my past, God used each step of the journey to strengthen me. There are many events in my past that have haunted me for years, but the Lord showed me that the key to being an over

Closing the Doors to Satan's Attacks: Overcoming Fear

comer is never allowing the enemy to use your past as a weapon against you. Whenever we give the enemy a place in our lives, we leave doors open for his attack. The attacks will come in many ways and without warning. Remember, Satan is a legalist and he knows his rights. When we leave a door open he can and will come in and wreak havoc in our homes, schools, children, jobs, marriages - wherever he is allowed. Let's not become "free range prey" for the enemy.

Recently, I discovered events from my past that were laying dormant waiting for Satan to use against me. I did not realize that these events had set up strongholds in my life. I forgot about them, but God did not and Satan certainly did not forget them because they fell into the realm of his territory. Satan is the accuser of the brethren and he will use un-confessed sin to attack us. Satan had the chains of my past in his hands and he also held the key. Never allow Satan to control your past, present or future because he will use it against you.

Closing the Doors to Satan's Attacks: Overcoming Fear

The Word of God says we are over comers by the blood of the Lamb and the word of our testimony. The Lord showed me that in the confession of our sins we are free from the chains of the past. Chains that have been binding us for years. Chains that Satan has on lock down to keep us from the fullness of God. Chains that bind us to pride, arrogance, un-forgiveness, anger, resentment, unbelief, mistrust, guilt, shame - the list could go on for miles.

I am going to share the most profound word the Lord spoke regarding fear and the residue associated with fear. Thank God for His mercy because Satan was using these strongholds to attack my health whenever I began to walk in my purpose and destiny. The Lord said, *I am teaching you how to break the constraints life has on you. This is the only way you will know and understand a deeper intimacy with me. As I guide you day by day there will be many things you do not understand, but know that they are for your good. It is necessary for where I am taking you. Remember the dream; I want you to remain seated in*

Closing the Doors to Satan's Attacks: Overcoming Fear

humility before My people. Never allow the enemy to bring fear into your life. Recognize it and take authority over it. The enemy is trying to bring discouragement to hinder you. He is also trying to bring doubt about your destiny. Do not fear the destiny that is ahead of you. The enemy is trying to use your consecration season to attack and shut down what is ahead. Go deeper into me because there you will find rest. The trial that is ahead I am using it to strengthen you. Know that I am there to lead and guide you. Finish the work I have set before you - so that you can move forward. You are not alone I am with you in every step. There is a tremendous press ahead and I am equipping you for it.

I cannot have the residue of your past becoming a place for Satan to hide. He would use the residue against you. This is the reason for the purging, it is uncomfortable, but it is necessary.

If I did not have faith in God I would not have written this book or any of the other books that God has given me.

Closing the Doors to Satan's Attacks: Overcoming Fear

There have been times when I wanted to give up because the road was tough. The circumstances of my past helped to develop the woman I am and the woman I am to become.

Closing the doors to Satan's attacks is a vital key to walking into your destiny. Jeremiah 29:11 tells us, *'For I know the plans that I have for you,' declares the LORD, 'plans for welfare and not for calamity to give you a future and a hope.* The Lord Jesus Christ holds the key to your destiny. Never allow Satan to kill, steal or destroy any aspect of your destiny. Never surrender your authority to the enemy, it is yours through the shed Blood of Jesus.

My journey has been an eye opening experience and I hope that my testimony will help others in their journey of discovering God's purpose and plan.

God is doing a new thing and He desires that we be a part of it. *Behold, I will do a new thing; now it shall spring forth; shall ye not know it? I will even make a way in the wilderness, and rivers in the desert* (Isaiah 43:19).

Closing the Doors to Satan's Attacks: Overcoming Fear

God wants to make a way in your wilderness and flow rivers in the desert of your life. This will require preparing ourselves through prayer, fasting and seeking the face of God. *And he said unto them, This kind can come forth by nothing, but by prayer and fasting* (Mark 9:29).

As we close the door on our deadliest enemy, the doors that are about to open to you no man can shut. *I know thy works: behold, I have set before thee an open door, and no man can shut* (Revelation 3:8).

Chapter 12
My Journey of Overcoming Fear
Study Guide

Exercise: Close the book and begin to seek the Lord for directions on beginning your journey of overcoming the fear in your life. Go to the appendix and search out scriptures dealing with fear and ask the Lord to show you areas hindered by fear. Use the space below to write out your own journey of overcoming fear. Remember, it may not be pleasant, but it is necessary for where God wants to take you.

_____
_____
_____
_____
_____
_____
_____
_____
_____

Closing the Doors to Satan's Attacks: Overcoming Fear

Chapter 13
Walking in Step with the Master

In order to fulfill the great commission, we must be in step with the Master. Walking in step with the Lord keeps us in the center of His will.

Direct my footsteps according to your word; let no sin rule over me. Redeem me from the oppression of men, that I may obey your precepts. Make your face shine upon your servant (Psalm 119:133-135).

Being in step with the Master requires we walk according to the Word of God. Listening at every instance for His direction for our path. It also means trusting Him in every area. There are several points that I believe are vital to staying in step with the Master.

Point #1:
The Lord has called us to a higher standard of living. Our walk must exemplify a Christ-Like lifestyle. Our very existence takes on an entirely new meaning as we receive

the revelation of WHO WE ARE IN CHRIST. If you are to walk in the Spirit, we must know who we are because it is vital to our spiritual growth. We must not allow the enemy to bind us to lives of mediocrity. *This I say then, walk in the Spirit, and ye shall not fulfil the lust of the flesh* (Galatians 5:16).

Point #2:

The prerequisites for walking in step with the Master involve a Psalm 139 petition before the Lord. When you ask the Lord to search your heart, trust me He will. What He reveals to you may not be what you were expecting, but it will set you on a course to walking in step with the Master.

> *O LORD, you have searched me and you know me. You know when I sit and when I rise; you perceive my thoughts from afar. You discern my going out and my lying down; you are familiar with all my ways* (Psalm 139:1-3).

Closing the Doors to Satan's Attacks: Overcoming Fear

Search me, O God, and know my heart; test me and know my anxious thoughts. See if there is any offensive way in me, and lead me in the way everlasting (Psalm 139:23-24).

Point #3
Unbelief is the worst hindrance to the move of God in your life. Unbelief is a demonic fruit that belongs to Satan and with unbelief comes disobedience to the commandments of God. When you allow unbelief to enter your heart, Satan has a legal right to attack you. Not only does it stop the flow of God's power, it also stops the flow of God's blessings. It also binds the individual to a life of mediocrity. Unbelief is equal to rebellion and no one can enter into the presence of the Lord with unbelief on his heart. Belief requires faith and without faith, it is impossible to please God, *"And without faith it is impossible to please God, because anyone who comes to him must believe that he exists and that he rewards those who earnestly seek him"* (Hebrews 11:6).

Point #4:

Trust is mandatory if you are to walk in step with the master.

> *Trust in the LORD with all thine heart; and lean not unto thine own understanding. In all thy ways acknowledge him, and he shall direct thy paths* (Proverbs 3:5-6).

Point #5:

If you are to walk in step with the Master you must agree with His Word. You must also be in agreement with His purpose and plan for your life. IT IS NOT ABOUT YOU!! *Can two walk together, except they be agreed* (Amos 3:3)?

> *For I know the plans I have for you, declares the LORD, plans to prosper you and not to harm you, plans to give you hope and a future. Then you will call Upon me and come and pray to me, and I will listen to you. You will seek me and find me when you seek me with all your heart* (Jeremiah 29:11-13).

Closing the Doors to Satan's Attacks: Overcoming Fear

God's plan for your life is far greater than any plan you could devise. His plan is perfect, just as His ways are perfect.

"For my thoughts are not your thoughts, neither are your ways my ways," declares the LORD. "As the heavens are higher than the earth, so are my ways higher than your ways and my thoughts than your thoughts (Isaiah 55:8-9).

Point #6:
Before you can begin walking in the Spirit, you must address questions that could hinder your walk now or in the future.

- I believe in God, but do I believe God?

- Is fear hindering your spiritual walk? (*2 Timothy 1:7*)

- Do I believe God for everyone else - EXCEPT ME? *(Ephesians 3:20)*

- How many times has God given you a directive and you were slow in acting it? *(Psalm 119:60)*

- Has God sent you a word and you allowed Satan to steal it with unbelief? *(Psalm 119:61)*

Closing the Doors to Satan's Attacks: Overcoming Fear

- When was the last time you shared Jesus? *(1 Peter 21)*

- When was the last time you sat listening for the Lord's voice?

- When was the last time the Lord instructed you to lay before Him and your biggest concern was what others would think? *(Proverbs 4:13)*

- What element paves the way for disobedience? *(Romans 4:20)*

- What is the biggest hindrance to hearing the voice of the Lord? *(Psalm 95:7-8)*

- What is the worst hindrance to the move of God in your life?

- What opens the door to spiritual laziness?

Closing the Doors to Satan's Attacks: Overcoming Fear

Scriptures to equip you in Walking in Step with the Master

It is vital to be armed and dangerous when it comes to spiritual warfare. *(For the weapons of our warfare are not carnal, but mighty through God to the pulling down of strong holds;) Casting down imaginations, and every high thing that exalteth itself against the knowledge of God, and bringing into captivity every thought to the obedience of Christ; And having in a readiness to revenge all disobedience, when your obedience is fulfilled.*

2 Corinthians 10:4-6

***My steps** have held to your paths; my feet have not slipped* (Psalm17:5).

*Righteousness goes before him and prepares the way for **his steps*** (Psalm 85:13).

*I have considered my ways and have turned **my steps to your statutes**. I will hasten and not delay to obey your commands* (Psalm 119:59-60).

Closing the Doors to Satan's Attacks: Overcoming Fear

*When you walk, **your steps** will not be hampered; when you run, you will not stumble. Hold on to instruction, do not let it go; guard it well, for it is your life. Do not set foot on the path of the wicked or walk in the way of evil men* (Proverbs 4:12-14).

*In his heart a man plans his course, but the LORD determines **his steps*** (Proverbs 16:9).

*A **man's steps** are directed by the LORD. How then can anyone understand his own way* (Proverbs 20:24)?

***My feet** have closely followed **his steps**; I have kept to his way without turning aside. I have not departed from the commands of his lips; I have treasured the words of his mouth more than my daily bread* (Job 23:11-12).

Closing the Doors to Satan's Attacks: Overcoming Fear

*To this you were called, because Christ suffered for you, leaving you an example, that you should follow in **his steps**. He committed no sin, and no deceit was found in his mouth"* (1Peter 2:21-22).

*He **staggered not at the promise of God** through unbelief; but was strong in faith, giving glory to God* (Romans 4:20).

The bible warns us to give no place to the devil. When we allow Satan a place in our lives, are we walking in step with him? Are we walking in the fruits of the Spirit or the fruits of Satan? We know that Satan came to kill, steal and destroy. Never stagger at the promises of God through unbelief, fear or doubt. Be strong in your faith because it gives God glory. Stay in step with the Master.

Walking in Step with the Master Means Knowing the Master

When you are walking in step with the Master it means you moving to a place of intimacy with the Father and pressing towards the mark of knowing His will for your life. When you are walking in step with the Master, you will find time to spend with Him and you will always seek to please Him.

Here are eight keys to knowing God:

KNOWING GOD MEANS
1. Spending quality time in His Word.
2. Spending quiet time meditating on His Word.
3. Spending time listening for Him.
4. Trusting Him when things look hopeless.
5. Worshipping Him.
6. A desire to be in His presence for who He is and not for what He can give you.
7. A hunger and passion for His presence.
8. Finally, knowing God means obeying Him.

Closing the Doors to Satan's Attacks: Overcoming Fear

Chapter 13
Walking in Step with the Master
Study Guide

1. Write out a brief analysis outline the points vital to staying in step with the Master.

_____
_____
_____
_____
_____
_____
_____
_____
_____
_____
_____
_____
_____
_____
_____

Closing the Doors to Satan's Attacks: Overcoming Fear

Closing the Doors to Satan's Attacks: Overcoming Fear

Before a believer can begin walking in the Spirit, you must address questions that could hinder his walk now or in the future.

2. I believe in God, but do I believe God?

_____
_____
_____
_____
_____
_____
_____
_____
_____
_____
_____
_____
_____
_____
_____
_____

Closing the Doors to Satan's Attacks: Overcoming Fear

3. What part does fear play in your spiritual walk? (2 Timothy 1:7)

_____
_____
_____
_____
_____
_____
_____
_____
_____
_____
_____
_____
_____
_____
_____
_____
_____
_____
_____

Closing the Doors to Satan's Attacks: Overcoming Fear

4. Do you believe God for everyone else - EXCEPT YOU? (Ephesians 3:20)

Closing the Doors to Satan's Attacks: Overcoming Fear

5. Has God sent you a word and you allowed Satan to steal it with unbelief?

Closing the Doors to Satan's Attacks: Overcoming Fear

6. When was the last time you sat listening for the Lord's voice?

7. What element paves the way for disobedience? (Romans 4:20).

Closing the Doors to Satan's Attacks: Overcoming Fear

8. Walking in step with the Master means that we get to know the Father.

Closing the Doors to Satan's Attacks: Overcoming Fear

9. Write out the eight keys to knowing God:

KNOWING GOD MEANS

a. _____

b. _____

c. _____

d. _____

e. _____

f. _____

g. _____

h. _____

Chapter 14
Faith: The Substance of Your Life

Faith is the substance of things hoped for, the evidence of things not seen (Hebrews 11:1). Many of us grew up with an attitude of the only things that matter in life are the things that we can see, taste or touch. Tangible things. Nevertheless, faith lives on a plane that the carnal mind cannot comprehend.

We teach and preach faith, but how many of us really walk in the level of faith that God desires for us? Faith is not a tangible substance that you can put your finger on. It is not a see it, touch it, taste it experience. Unfortunately, many believers miss one of the most awesome experiences in a Christian's life when they sit around waiting for God to move. They make statements like, "God told me to teach His word, but I am waiting for Him to give me an assignment." What about the Sunday school class that is in need of a teacher? God promised you a business, but instead of following the wisdom of Habakkuk 2:2-3, *Write the vision, and make it plain upon tables, that he may run that readeth it. For the vision is yet for an appointed time, but at the end it shall speak, and not lie: though it tarry, wait for it; because it will surely come, it will not tarry,* you sit around waiting for a business to drop out of the sky.

Not long ago, the Lord told me to tell a young couple to start packing because He was giving them a new home. The husband replied, *"I am not going to pack until I see a house with my own eyes."* Instead of believing God for the new home, they settled for a house that God did not choose. It was a disaster from the start. They lasted in the house less than a year and had to move. *So then faith cometh by hearing, and hearing by the word of God* (Romans 10:17). To whom are you listening?

When we begin the journey of walking in faith and walking away from fear, we can trust God and His Word even when everything seems impossible. Many things in

Closing the Doors to Satan's Attacks: Overcoming Fear

life seems so far out of reach and so overwhelming to our finite minds. It is virtually impossible to comprehend the depth of God's love for us. I say this because if we really understood God's eternal love for us, we would do many things differently. God said in Psalms 84:11, *No good thing does He withhold from those who walk uprightly* (NASB). He is saying that he will bless us if we walk upright and stand on the strength of His word. That means walking in faith and not in fear. Trusting every word that proceeds from His mouth. Standing unmovable and unshakable on His word and His promises.

As you begin to close the door to the fear in your life and open the door to faith, you will begin to discover a deeper level in your relationship with the Lord.

Closing the door to fear means closing the door to Satan's attacks against you. When the door of fear is closed and you begin to walk in the newness of your journey you will find a level of trust and guidance like never before.

Closing the Doors to Satan's Attacks: Overcoming Fear

As I mentioned at the beginning of this chapter, we teach and preach faith, but how many believers really walk in the level of faith God desires for us? In Matthew 17:20 Jesus talks about the nature of true faith. The faith Jesus desires for us is the kind of faith that can move mountains. It is a level of faith that heals the sick, raises the dead and casts out demons. Can our fragile human minds grab hold to the depth of faith Jesus speaks about?

When I began my journey of walking in faith and walking away from fear, I discovered key elements vital to moving to a deeper level of faith. Look at the following scriptures and you can clearly see how faith is an essential part of your daily walk with the Lord.

➤ **Faith produces results**
- *...mountain, Remove hence to yonder place* (Matthew 17:20).

➤ **Faith in God**
- *And Jesus answering saith unto them, Have faith in God* (Mark 11:22).

Closing the Doors to Satan's Attacks: Overcoming Fear

➢ **Faith begins in the heart.**
- *...straightway the father of the child cried out, and said with tears, Lord, I believe; help thou mine unbelief* (Mark 9:24).

Faith is a move that begins in the heart of the believer. In Mark 9:24 the father of the demon possessed child asked Jesus for the strength to believe. The strength to believe begins in the heart and is given to us by the Holy Spirit.

➢ **Faith draws us closer to God.**
- *Let us draw near with a true heart in full assurance of faith* (Hebrews 10:22).

➢ **Faith begin and ends with Jesus**
- *Looking unto Jesus the author and finisher of our faith; who for the joy that was set before him endured the cross, despising the shame, and is set down at the right hand of the throne of God* (Hebrews 12:2).

Closing the Doors to Satan's Attacks: Overcoming Fear

Hebrews 12:2 tells us that Jesus is the Author and Finisher of our faith. Therefore, every aspect of our faith begins and ends with Him. Apart from Him we are nothing and we can do nothing.

- **A measure of faith is given to each of us**
  - *For by the grace given me I say to every one of you: Do not think of yourself more highly than you ought, but rather think of yourself with sober judgment, in accordance with the measure of faith God has given you* (Romans 12:3).

God gave every man a measure of faith, therefore faith is ultimately under God's control.

- **God knows our hearts**
  - *And put no difference between us and them, purifying their hearts by faith* (Acts 15:9).

God knows our heart and He sees the faith in us. He purifies our hearts with an inward work of regeneration by the Holy Spirit.

Closing the Doors to Satan's Attacks: Overcoming Fear

> **We are kept by power of God through faith**
> - *Who are kept by the power of God through faith unto salvation ready to be revealed in the last time (1 Peter 1:5).*

First Peter 1:5 assures us that we are kept by the power of God through our faith. We are protected against Satan's attacks which are out to steal, kill and destroy our lives. We must have faith if we are to be under God's protection. Our faith is the key to our salvation and salvation brings God's protection.

> **We are saved through Faith**
> - *That if thou shalt confess with thy mouth the Lord Jesus, and shalt believe in thine heart that God hath raised him from the dead, thou shalt be saved (Romans 10:9).*

It is only through faith in Jesus Christ that we are saved. This is a believing in your heart kind of faith.

We must have NOW faith

- *Now faith is the substance of things hoped for, the evidence of things not seen* (Hebrews 11:1).

[**Reflection:** Read the entire chapter of Hebrews 11]

Now faith is the substance of things hoped for, the evidence of things not seen (Hebrews 11:1 KJV)

Now faith is the assurance of things hoped for, the conviction of things not seen (Hebrews 11:1 NASB).

NOW FAITH is the assurance (the confirmation, the title deed) of the things [we] hope for, being the proof of things [we] do not see and the conviction of their reality [faith perceiving as real fact what is not revealed to the senses] (Hebrews 11:1 AMP).

Now faith is assurance of things hoped for, a conviction of things not seen (Hebrews 11:1 ASV).

Closing the Doors to Satan's Attacks: Overcoming Fear

Hebrews chapter eleven speaks of a level of faith that requires an intensity of believing that is without compromise or constraints. In other words, trusting God in every situation. *"Now faith"* means we are steadfast to God and His word. Chapter eleven demonstrates that faith is trust in God in all circumstances…at all times.

A faith that:[5]
- Believes in spiritual realities (v. 1)
- Leads to righteousness (v. 4)
- Seeks God (v. 6)
- Believes in God's goodness (v. 6)
- Has confidence in God's Word (v. 7, 11)
- Obeys His commands (v. 8)
- Regulates life on His promises (v. 13, 39)
- Rejects the spirit of this present age (v. 13)
- Seeks a heavenly home (v. 14-16)
- Perseveres in testing (v. 17-19)
- Blesses the next generation (v. 21)
- Refuses the pleasures of sin (v. 25)
- Endures persecution (v. 27)

Closing the Doors to Satan's Attacks: Overcoming Fear

- Performs acts of righteousness (v. 33-35)
- Suffers for God (v. 25, 35-38)
- Does not return to "that country from whence they came out," i.e. the world. (v. 15-16)[6]

As you read Hebrews chapter eleven, I pray that every aspect of the chapter becomes a part of your every day life. As I stated earlier, *"Now faith"* means we are steadfast to God and His word.

Steadfast means:
- ✓ firm and unwavering in purpose, loyalty or resolve
- ✓ fixed: firmly fixed or constant

Unshakable means:
- ✓ firm and certain: not subject to doubt or uncertainty

Unmovable means:
- ✓ sticking firmly to an opinion or decision
- ✓ Unbothered or unaffected

Closing the Doors to Satan's Attacks: Overcoming Fear

Each of these words describes the plane our faith must live on. When our faith moves from level to level, we will see each trial and tribulation as stepping stones to greater faith.

> *When Jesus heard this, he was astonished and said to those following him, "I tell you the truth, I have not found anyone in Israel with such **great faith*** (Matthew 8:10).

> *Then Jesus answered, "Woman, you have **great faith**! Your request is granted." And her daughter was healed from that very hour* (Matthew 15:28).

> *Those who have served well gain an excellent standing and great assurance in their faith in Christ Jesus* (1 Timothy 3:13).

> *Faith is the substance of things hoped for, the evidence of things not seen* (Hebrews 11:1).

Closing the Doors to Satan's Attacks: Overcoming Fear

1 Peter 1:7 tells us, *That the trial of your faith, being much more precious than of gold that perisheth, though it be tried with fire, might be found unto praise and honour and glory at the appearing of Jesus Christ* (KJV).

The Amplified Version states, *So that [the genuineness] of your faith may be tested, [your faith] which is infinitely more precious than the perishable gold which is tested and purified by fire. [This proving of your faith is intended] to redound to [your] praise and glory and honor when Jesus Christ (the Messiah, the Anointed One) is revealed.*

Your faith is precious to God and as you go through the trials that come to test your faith, though the fire seems to be turned up twenty times hotter, the proving of your faith will be found to result in praise, glory and honor when our Lord and Savior Jesus Christ is revealed.

Hold on to one of the most precious gifts in the world, faith. With faith you can move mountains and change a nation.

Closing the Doors to Satan's Attacks: Overcoming Fear

- ✓ With faith you will please God.
- ✓ With faith you will give glory and honor to God.
- ✓ With faith you have the strength to endure.
- ✓ With faith you will lead others to Christ.
- ✓ With faith no road will seem too rough.
- ✓ With faith no mountain will be too high.
- ✓ With faith no river will be too wide.
- ✓ With faith no valley in life will be too low.

Never allow the enemy to steal your faith through fear, doubt or unbelief. *Be strong and of a good courage, fear not, nor be afraid of them: for the LORD thy God, he it is that doth go with thee; he will not fail thee, nor forsake thee* (Deuteronomy 31:6). As you close the doors to Satan's attacks know that the Lord is with you. He will never leave you nor forsake you.

For the LORD will not forsake his people for his great name's sake: because it hath pleased the LORD to make you his people (1Samuel 12:22).

I will never leave thee, nor forsake thee (Hebrews 13:5).

Closing the Doors to Satan's Attacks: Overcoming Fear

I pray that through this book you will begin the task of closing the doors to Satan's attacks. I pray you will find rest and peace for your heart through the pages of this book. Remember, you are not alone. Get ready for your study session.

Chapter 14
Faith: The Substance of Your Life
Study Guide

1. *Faith is the substance of things hoped for, the evidence of things not seen.* How does this verse apply to your life? (Hebrews 11:1)

_____
_____
_____
_____
_____
_____
_____
_____
_____
_____
_____
_____
_____

Closing the Doors to Satan's Attacks: Overcoming Fear

2. God said in Psalm 84:11, *No good thing does He withhold from those who walk uprightly.* Does this apply to you? Why?

_____
_____
_____
_____
_____
_____
_____
_____
_____
_____
_____
_____
_____
_____
_____

Closing the Doors to Satan's Attacks: Overcoming Fear

3. In Matthew 17:20 Jesus talks about the nature of true faith. The faith Jesus desires for us is the kind of faith that can move mountains. A level of faith that heals the sick raises the dead and casts out demons. Can our fragile human minds grab hold to the depth of faith Jesus speaks about?

_____
_____
_____
_____
_____
_____
_____
_____
_____
_____
_____
_____
_____
_____

4. What are the key elements vital to moving to a deeper level of faith?

  ➢ Example: **Faith produces results**

  ...mountain, Remove hence to yonder place (Matthew 17:20)

Closing the Doors to Satan's Attacks: Overcoming Fear

Closing the Doors to Satan's Attacks: Overcoming Fear

5. Read the entire chapter of Hebrews 11. Write out Hebrews 11:1.

Closing the Doors to Satan's Attacks: Overcoming Fear

6. *"Now faith"* means we are steadfast to God and His word. Chapter 11 demonstrates that faith is trust in God in all circumstances…at all times. It is a faith that:

1) _____
2) _____
3) _____
4) _____
5) _____
6) _____
7) _____
8) _____
9) _____
10) _____
11) _____
12) _____
13) _____
14) _____
15) _____
16) _____

Closing the Doors to Satan's Attacks: Overcoming Fear

7. Define the following terms:

Steadfast means:

___

Unshakable means:

___

Unmovable means:

___

Closing the Doors to Satan's Attacks: Overcoming Fear

8. Write out a scripture that best defines great faith. Use the ones in the chapter or search out additional scriptures on your own.

_____
_____
_____
_____
_____
_____
_____
_____
_____

9. Hold on to one of the most precious gifts, faith. With faith you can move mountains and change a nation.

Through faith:

_____
_____
_____
_____

Closing the Doors to Satan's Attacks: Overcoming Fear

_____

_____

_____

_____

_____

10. As you close the doors to Satan's attacks know that the Lord is with you. *He will never leave you nor forsake you.* What does this mean to you? How can you apply it to your life?

_____

_____

_____

_____

_____

_____

_____

_____

_____

_____

Chapter 15
I'm Living the Last Chapter

The title of this chapter speaks for itself. November 11, 2008 is the date I started living the last chapter.

I thought the journey of writing this book had come to an end until November 11, 2008 when my husband, Gregg was rear-ended by an 18-wheel tractor-trailer.

The last chapter began after the twenty-one day consecration I mentioned earlier. Gregg was on his way to men's Tuesday Night Prayer at It Is Written Ministries. Traffic was at a stand still when suddenly a tractor trailer came barreling down I-35 northbound and failed to stop. Crashing into Gregg's van and sending him into another vehicle. Gregg was rendered semi-conscious and paramedics had to come to his rescue.

Closing the Doors to Satan's Attacks: Overcoming Fear

After being extricated from the van, he was rushed to the hospital where they began the examinations, while keeping him immobilized for fear of spinal injuries. They found internal bleeding, neck and back trauma and other injuries. Later, they discovered an Achilles tendon injury that required a leg cast.

This is the day I began living the last chapter of this book. The affairs of the ministry fell on me, as well as the household needs, business, and finances and just about everything you can possibly think of. Not to mention family members in their concern for my husband put added pressure on me to have answers to every question.

When times like this hit you in the face you had better have on the whole armor of God. When the enemy comes in like a flood… Well the enemy came in like a flood raging against me and the only thing I remember is the voice of the Lord saying, *"you are about to go through a storm…"* I could hear the words as I felt the weight of everything bearing down on me. Somewhere in the midst

Closing the Doors to Satan's Attacks: Overcoming Fear

of it all, the enemy found a crack in my foundation which resulted in an attack of high blood pressure. It came from the stress of going through such a devastating time - **I was living the last chapter.**

To make matters worse, depression crept in. I didn't realize that the spirit of depression was trying to creep in through the crack in my foundation [high blood pressure.] I also noticed that I was picking up weight which came from stress eating. Stress eating is eating when you are not hungry in order to relieve the pressure. With each stressful encounter, I found myself reaching for food as a way to comfort myself and relieve tension. It was the Lord in His gentle and loving way who pointed it out. One day after receiving more distressing news, the Holy Spirit said, *"do you see what you are doing? You are eating again after you received stressful news. You are not hungry you are trying to cope with your situation."* The revelation hit me like a ton of bricks. I was stress eating for no apparent reason other the pressure was weighing me down.

Closing the Doors to Satan's Attacks: Overcoming Fear

Before we go any further get this in your spirit.
1. The weight of my circumstances lead to - **STRESS.**
2. Stress lead to **OVEREATING.**
3. Overeating lead to **WEIGHT GAIN.**
4. Weight gain lead to **HIGH BLOOD PRESSURE.**
5. They all contributed to **DEPRESSION.**

Did you see that? With each crack in my foundation, the enemy, Satan could burrow deeper into my circumstances. What now? Pray and pray now! I had to get on my face and in God's face for the direction out of this HOT MESS!

The situations in my life seem to snow ball and I needed to seek a doctor for help with the high blood pressure. I had my blood pressure checked and the test showed 161 over 123. Absolutely too high and too dangerous. Do you see how in a matter of a few months the enemy can infiltrate your life and turn it up side down? He can and he will if he is allowed permission to do so.

Closing the Doors to Satan's Attacks: Overcoming Fear

This marked the beginning of my spiritual battle to reclaim everything the enemy sought to kill, steal or destroy.

I spent a lot of time on my face seeking God's face for the answers needed to bring me through. Remember, the Lord had given me warning about the storm that was ahead. I must admit that I had no idea He meant a storm of this magnitude, a virtual tsunami.

The greater your faith, the greater your trials. The Lord **allows** greater trials to take you to a place of greater faith. The place I am in today in no way resembles my place of faith in 2007 and certainly does not resemble the place of faith in 2001.

One night while on my face, the Lord said, *"Your trial like that of Job's is over."*

Gregg has recovered from his injuries and the doctors said he is blessed to be alive. His faith has grown significantly

Closing the Doors to Satan's Attacks: Overcoming Fear

through this journey and he has watched God move on his behalf in some amazing ways. Our marriage is stronger, as well as our friendship.

Staying close to the Lord is the only remedy for overcoming Satan's attacks. The trials and tribulations will make your stronger or they might even break you down in order for God to rebuild you into His image. Whatever the case may be, it is a tool God will use. What Satan means for bad in your life, God will turn it around for your good and His glory.

You will have to walk out the final chapter of the pages of your journey in order for the Lord to:
1. Strengthen your faith.
2. Show you the strongholds in your life.
3. Get your attention.
4. Break off fear.
5. Move you to another level in your journey.

Closing the Doors to Satan's Attacks: Overcoming Fear

In living the last chapter the Lord allowed me to see areas in my mental, physical and spiritual life that needed strengthening. The strength to endure begins with deeper prayer, faith and trust in Him. *Without faith it is impossible to please Him, for he who comes to God must believe that He is and that He is a rewarder of those who seek Him* (Hebrews 11:6). As you journey through the valley of the shadow of... fear nothing and trust God for everything. *For God hath not given us the spirit of fear; but of power, and of love, and of a sound mind* (2 Timothy 1:7).

Even if you never write a book, there will come a time when you will have to live out a chapter in your life that will change your life and challenge everything you thought you knew about life, faith and inner strength. As you journey from valley to valley, mountain to mountain and glory to glory, you will begin to discover the awesome power of our Lord and Savior as He fights the battle in your life. Your mandate is to close the doors to Satan's attacks by taking authority over every area of

Closing the Doors to Satan's Attacks: Overcoming Fear

fear. When fear rears its ugly head, you must cut it off before it has an opportunity to take root. There are things in life that we will have to face head on. As you face the giants in your life "move forward" and do not look back with full assurance of the ONE who leads you, Jehovah Rohi, The Lord Our Shepherd.

As a child I had a fear of horses and would not go near a horse. When I became an adult I decided that the best way to overcome my fear of horses was to face it. So I went to a horseback riding ranch and took lessons. The first day there the horse looked menacing and my first thought was to run, but I stayed, mounted the horse and I have been riding ever since. Some areas of fear must be faced head on. Just do it scared and fear will leave you. Remember, *For God did not give us a spirit of timidity (of cowardice, of craven and cringing and fawning fear), but [He has given us a spirit] of power and of love and of calm and well-balanced mind and discipline and self-control* (2 Timothy 1:7 AMP).

Closing the Doors to Satan's Attacks: Overcoming Fear

Close the doors to Satan's attacks by closing the door of fear in your life. As you close each door, the Lord will open a door to a victorious life through Christ Jesus. The battle is the Lords and the victory is ours. Walk through every door the Lord opens for you - no fear and no doubt.

This is the last chapter of this book, but not the last chapter of your journey. We must keep the doors closed against Satan's attacks by staying in the Lord's presence. We must trust in the Lord to deliver us out of every trial. The Bible says it will rain on the just and the unjust in Matthew 5:45: *That ye may be the children of your Father which is in heaven: for he maketh his sun to rise on the evil and on the good, and sendeth rain on the just and on the unjust* (KJV). In knowing this, we must not allow the enemy to overtake us with lies and deceptions - give no place to the devil. Instead, let us trust in the Lord; stand on the Rock of our Salvation and FEAR NOT! For the Lord is with us ready to bring a great harvest and a great victory in our lives.

Closing the Doors to Satan's Attacks: Overcoming Fear

You will find that keeping the doors closed will be a never ending journey because the enemy is out to hinder any work done for Kingdom of God. Because fear is one of his best weapons against us, he will continue to use it against us. He is always looking for cracks in our foundation. He is always searching for a weapon to use against us, but no weapon formed against us shall prosper. As long as we continue to press forward for the advancement of the Kingdom of God, the Lord will be there to fight on our behalf.

Just as the Lord told Moses while the children of Israel were standing at the Red Sea, *then the LORD said to Moses, "Why are you crying out to Me? Tell the sons of Israel to go forward* (Exodus 14:15). The Lord is ready to work on your behalf so what are you waiting for? **Fear not**, the Lord is your shield, and your exceeding great reward. **Move forward!**

Fear not, O land; be glad and rejoice: for the LORD will do great things.

Joel 2:21

Closing the Doors to Satan's Attacks: Overcoming Fear

Closing the Doors to Satan's Attacks: Overcoming Fear

Growth Exercises

Exercise #1:

Write out a prayer for binding the Spirit of Fear over your life. Remember pray God's Word back to Him.

Here is an example: *Strongman called Spirit of Fear, I bind you in the Name of Jesus Christ along with all your works, roots, fruits, links and spirits that are in my life and the lives of everybody I have prayed for today, along with all of your fruits and spirits of...and send back to the pit of hell. In Jesus Name.*

_____
_____
_____
_____
_____
_____
_____
_____
_____
_____
_____

Closing the Doors to Satan's Attacks: Overcoming Fear

Closing the Doors to Satan's Attacks: Overcoming Fear

Exercise #2:

Write out a prayer using Hebrews 11:1 as your foundation.

Closing the Doors to Satan's Attacks: Overcoming Fear

Exercise #3:

Write out a prayer for binding the Spirit of Confusion over your life. Remember pray God's Word back to Him. Here is an example: *Strongman called Spirit of Confusion, I bind you in the Name of Jesus Christ along with all your works, roots, fruits, links and spirits that are in my life and the lives of everybody I have prayed for today, along with all of your fruits and spirits of...*

_____
_____
_____
_____
_____
_____
_____
_____
_____
_____
_____
_____

Closing the Doors to Satan's Attacks: Overcoming Fear

Closing the Doors to Satan's Attacks: Overcoming Fear

Exercise #4:

Write out a prayer for loosing the Spirit of Peace and sound Mind over your life. Remember pray God's Word back to Him. Begin with 2 Timothy 1:7.

Closing the Doors to Satan's Attacks: Overcoming Fear

Exercise #5:

Read James 1:2-6

Consider it pure joy, my brothers, whenever you face trials of many kinds, because you know that the testing of your faith develops perseverance. Perseverance must finish its work so that you may be mature and complete, not lacking anything. If any of you lacks wisdom, he should ask God, who gives generously to all without finding fault, and it will be given to him. But when he asks, he must believe and not doubt, because he who doubts is like a wave of the sea, blown and tossed by the wind.

Explain the verses as they pertain to your life. How can James make you stronger?

_____
_____
_____
_____
_____
_____
_____

Closing the Doors to Satan's Attacks: Overcoming Fear

Closing the Doors to Satan's Attacks: Overcoming Fear

Exercise #6:

Write out a prayer for binding any spirit over your family. Remember pray God's Word back to Him. Be specific when listing the spirits: such as drugs, alcoholism, lust, greed, etc. Be sure to speak the person's name as you bind the spirit. Once you have bound the spirit be sure loose the fruit of the Lord's Spirit over them as well:

(Example: Binding Fear)
I bind you Spirit of Fear in the Name of Jesus along with all your roots, works, fruits, links, and spirits that are in my life, (my children, husband, other family members) and the lives of everyone I have prayed for today. In the Name of Jesus I bind you and loose you from me and my children, husband, other family members and everyone I have prayed for today. By the blood of Jesus I command you not to come back into our presence ever again. I ask you, Heavenly Father, In the Name of Jesus to loose into me and each person I have prayed for to receive Power, Love and A Sound Mind according to Second Timothy 1:7. In Jesus Christ Holy and Righteous Name. Amen.

Closing the Doors to Satan's Attacks: Overcoming Fear

Closing the Doors to Satan's Attacks: Overcoming Fear

Closing the Doors to Satan's Attacks: Overcoming Fear

Exercise: #7:

What will you do from this day forward to close the doors to Satan's attacks against you?

_____
_____
_____
_____
_____
_____
_____
_____
_____
_____
_____
_____
_____
_____
_____
_____
_____

Closing the Doors to Satan's Attacks: Overcoming Fear

FEAR NOT!
Scriptures

Here are several scriptures to encourage your heart when faced with fear. Pray these scriptures and hide them in your heart

After these things the word of the LORD came unto Abram in a vision, saying, Fear not, Abram: I am thy shield, and thy exceeding great reward. Genesis 15:1

And the LORD appeared unto him the same night, and said, I am the God of Abraham thy father: fear not, for I am with thee, and will bless thee, and multiply thy seed for my servant Abraham's sake. Genesis 26:24

Behold, the LORD thy God hath set the land before thee: go up and possess it, as the LORD God of thy fathers hath said unto thee; fear not, neither be discouraged. Deuteronomy 1:21

Closing the Doors to Satan's Attacks: Overcoming Fear

Be strong and of a good courage, fear not, nor be afraid of them: for the LORD thy God, he it is that doth go with thee; he will not fail thee, nor forsake thee. Deuteronomy 31:6

And David said to Solomon his son, Be strong and of good courage, and do it: fear not, nor be dismayed: for the LORD God, even my God, will be with thee; he will not fail thee, nor forsake thee, until thou hast finished all the work for the service of the house of the LORD. 1 Chronicles 28:20

Ye shall not need to fight in this battle: set yourselves, stand ye still, and see the salvation of the LORD with you, O Judah and Jerusalem: fear not, nor be dismayed; tomorrow go out against them: for the LORD will be with you. 2 Chronicles 20:17

And fear not them which kill the body, but are not able to kill the soul: but rather fear him which is able to destroy both soul and body in hell. Matthew 10:28

Closing the Doors to Satan's Attacks: Overcoming Fear

Prayer of Salvation
~~~~~~~~~~~~~~~~~~~~~~~~~~~~

No matter what you do in life, nothing else will matter except your relationship with Jesus Christ. A committed relationship with Jesus is the key to a victorious life. Our Lord and Savior laid down His life for us. He rose again for us so that we could spend eternity with Him. Jesus said, *"I am come that they might have life, and that they might have it more abundantly."*

It is God's will that everyone receive eternal salvation. The only way to receive salvation is to call upon the name of Jesus and confess Him as Lord of your life. The Bible says in Romans 10:9-13, *that if thou shalt confess with thy mouth the Lord Jesus, and shalt believe in thine heart that God hath raised him from the dead, thou shalt be saved. For with the heart man believeth unto righteousness; and with the mouth confession is made unto salvation. For the scripture saith, whosoever believeth on him shall not be ashamed. For there is no difference between the Jew and the Greek: for the same Lord over all is rich unto all that call upon him. For whosoever shall call upon the name of the Lord shall be saved.*

God loves you, no matter who you are, no matter what your past. God loves you so much that He gave His one and only begotten Son for you. The Bible tells us *"...whoever believes in him shall not perish but have eternal life"* (John 3:16 NIV). Jesus laid down His life and rose again so that we could spend eternity with Him in heaven and experience His absolute best on earth. If you would like to receive Jesus into your life, say the following prayer aloud. It is vital that you mean it from your heart.

> ***Heavenly Father, I come to You admitting that I am a sinner. Right now, I choose to turn away from sin, and I ask You to cleanse me of all unrighteousness. I believe that Your Son, Jesus, died on the cross to take away my sins. I also believe that He rose again from the dead so that I may be justified and made righteous through faith in Him. I call upon the name of Jesus Christ to be***

Closing the Doors to Satan's Attacks: Overcoming Fear

the Savior of my life. Jesus, I choose to follow You, and I ask that You fill me with the power of the Holy Spirit. I declare right now that I am a born-again child of God. I am free from sin, and full of the righteousness of God. I am saved in Jesus' name. Amen.

If you prayed this prayer to receive Jesus Christ as your Lord and Savior or if this book has blessed your life, we would like to hear from you. Please write us:

Igniting the Fire Publishing
1314 North 38th Street, Suite 101
Kansas City, KS 66102
Or
It Is Written Ministries
1314 North 38th Street, Suite 102
Kansas City, KS 66102

Meet Dr. Jacquie

The Author

Dr. Jacquelyn Brown-Hadnot is an author and teacher whose passion is to teach the bible in a way that changes lives. She has written several books such as the award winning *Cry Aloud, Spare Not! A Prophetic Call to the Fast God Has Chosen for You*, which received the 2007 Indie Excellence Finalist Award and USA Book News 2006 Best General Religion Book of the Year.

The Pastor

It is her great love for the Body of Christ that prompted Jacquie to birth It Is Written Ministries, Inc. It Is Written Ministries is a unique non-profit ministry that endeavors to encourage, motivate, and educate individuals to walk in wisdom, character, and holiness. It Is Written feeds the triune man; mind, body and spirit through outreaches such as food and clothing pantries, nursing home outreaches, meals to the homeless and teaching ministries on foundations for victorious Christian living, biblical financial principles, prayer and worship.

She is the founder of the Agape Learning Center, an outreach of It Is Written Ministries. The learning center was founded to provide a quality education to individuals with a desire to grow in their personal lives, but cannot afford a traditional education.

The Teacher / Speaker

Dr. Jacquie is a frequently requested speaker for churches, women's groups, general audiences, and seminars for independent gospel artists, biblical financial principals, fasting, prayer and worship.

She holds a Doctorate in Pastoral Theology, a Masters in Ministry Leadership and Bachelors in Theology.

Jacquie has made numerous television appearances and she is also the host of *Light for Your Path* and *The Heart of a Psalmist* radio broadcasts that air nationally and internationally in more than 56 countries, 80+ cities.

Closing the Doors to Satan's Attacks: Overcoming Fear

The Psalmist

Jacquie flows under a powerful three-fold evangelistic, psalmist and prophetic anointing causing her to be an effective vessel for the Kingdom of God. Jacquie is a Spoken Word Psalmist and her CD "His Mercy Endures Forever" has received nationwide airplay and won numerous awards. She has released two additional worship projects, The Spoken Word of Love and The Extravagant Love of God.

Jacquie frequently ministers music where she speaks. As a psalmist music is a vital part of worship. Jacquie uses music as a way to connect to the heart of God's people.

The Entrepreneur

Jacquie and her husband Minister Gregory Hadnot launched Igniting the Fire Media Group in 2006.

Jacquie has been the President and CFO of The Diversified Group, Inc. an accounting and income preparation firm for over twenty six years.

Closing the Doors to Satan's Attacks: Overcoming Fear

Jacquie and Minister Gregory have been married for over tem years and together they oversee It Is Written Ministries. They reside in Overland Park, KS. She has one daughter, Jacquanda and a grandson, Tristan.

Closing the Doors to Satan's Attacks: Overcoming Fear

Other Books & Materials by Dr. Jacquie

Books in Print
- The Extravagant Love of God: Experiencing the Prophetic Flow
- Cry Aloud, Spare Not! A Prophetic Call to the Fast God Has Chosen
- Cry Aloud, Spare Not! The Companion-Study Guide
- His Mercy Endures Forever: Psalms, Prayers & Meditations
- To Make War with the Saints; Satan's Kingdom Agenda
- A Treasure in the Pleasure of Loving God
- Loving God through His Names: 365 Days of the Year
- Closing the Doors to Satan's Attacks: *Overcoming Fear*
- Where Is Your God? Have We Lost the Referential Fear of the Lord?

Audio Books & Teachings
- More of You... (Volume 1)
- In the Face of Adversity: *Overcoming Life's Storms*
- Be Not Deceived...
- Where Is Your God?
- Recognizing Your Due Season
- Praying the Healing Scriptures
- The Enemy in Me: *Overcoming Self-Life Issues*
- Trusting God in a Season of Discouragement
- The Harlot Heart

Music
- The Extravagant Love of God
- His Mercy Endures Forever: Praying the Psalms
- The Spoken Word of Love

DVD
- When Your Faith is Being Tested
- Agents of Change

Closing the Doors to Satan's Attacks: Overcoming Fear

For More Information:
www.jacquiehadnot.com
www.ignitingthefire.net
Or write us:
jacquie@jacquiehadnot.com

Bibliography

1 Cry Aloud, Spare Not! A Prophetic Call to the Fast God Has Chosen for You, Dr. Jacquelyn Hadnot

2 A Treasure in the Pleasure of Loving God, Dr. Jacquelyn Hadnot, 2007

3 The New Scofield Study Bible, Oxford University Press, pp. 1769

4 Life In the Spirit Study Bible, Zondervan, pp 1974

5 Life In the Spirit Study Bible, Zondervan, pp 1974

www.ingramcontent.com/pod-product-compliance
Lightning Source LLC
LaVergne TN
LVHW051827080426
835512LV00018B/2751